Trends in Linguistics

State-of-the-Art Reports

edited by

W. Winter

University of Kiel, Germany

1

STANDARD ITALIAN

by

GIORGIO RAIMONDO CARDONA

1976

MOUTON

THE HAGUE - PARIS

ISBN 90 279 3055 4

Printed in the Netherlands

TABLE OF CONTENTS

FOREWORD

Students of Italian linguistics are lucky enough to have such useful reference books at their disposal as Hall (1958a; *Bibliografia della linguistica italiana*), a monumental bibliography of every item pertaining to the field, and Muljačić (1971; *Introduzione allo studio della lingua italiana*), a practical introduction to extant literature.

These two books are different in scope as well in size: Hall (1958a) pursues a full coverage of the area, but, on principle, gives only titles. Sometimes he adds a quick comment when quoting a review and mentions its tenor. The first supplement volume published in 1969, covers Italian studies through 1966 (see now Hall 1973).

Muljačić (1971a) is more compact; he introduces topics critically and sometimes expounds them in detail. His book abounds with much background information on Italian studies such as subsidiary if not proper linguistic tools, forthcoming books, reports on work in progress and so on, and obviously is more up-to-date than Hall.

The two works supplement each other and used together they provide an excellent introduction to Italian studies.

The aim of the present survey is not to compete with Hall and Muljačić, which would hardly be possible, but rather to present in an extremely reduced space a brief outline of the development of Italian linguistic studies, sketching the chief trends, the prevailing lines of interest, pointing out the main gaps to be breached and analyzing the failures.

In limiting the choice of items to be discussed in the text and the bibliography, I have relied on two criteria: (1) usefulness from the point of view of factual evidence, and/or (2) theoretical and methodological interest. Obviously, an item which fails to satisfy at least one of these prerequisites, hardly deserves to be quoted. But, perhaps, Occam's razor ought to have been used more drastically.

The bibliography appended to the text (it might seem that the text is prefixed to the bibliography!) aims to give a rather fair idea of what has been published in the field of Italian studies in the 20th century; occasionally, important contributions in older works are also mentioned.

The arrangement of topics was a crucial point. My initial idea was to establish a solid theoretical framework and then to treat the topics within it. But scientific literature does not develop in accordance with a theoretical framework, and I foun it more satisfactory to begin directly with the main topics and let the framework form itself as data fell into place around the main poles. Leaving aside some obvio overlapping, this inner arrangement is by no means unbiased, but I hope that my biases will not negatively influence the whole.

I am deeply indebted to Prof. W. Winter, who was kind enough to accept this contribution first for his *Series critica* and now for inclusion in the new series *Trends in Linguistics*, and to Susan E. Zerad Garau, who has patiently looked through my text, improving my non-native English. Obviously, any remaining errors are my own.

Istituto di Glottologia   (1975)
Università di Roma

INTRODUCTION

Till very recent times the synchronic approach has been neglected, on the whole, by Italian scholars.

Owing to a tradition of prevailingly historical studies, the main bulk of research was focused on the problems of older phases of Italian, and attention was paid to the Origins, the Middle Ages, the Renaissance, and only occasionally to more recent stages. It is not irrelevant that every linguist, even if specialized in some other field, was expected to contribute at least once or twice in his academic career to Old Italian: but the same is not true for more recent phases of Italian.

Nobody should complain about that, since this unceasing tradition has produced an excellent amount of research on various aspects of Old Italian, carried out by such outstanding scholars as Baldelli, Castellani, Dardano, Folena, Migliorini, Monteverdi, Segre, Schiaffini, to quote just a few names (the essays of some of them have been collected in special volumes, which allows us to have a quick glimpse at their activity; see Baldelli 1971, Monteverdi 1971, Segre 1963a).

In view of the relatively young age of Italian descriptive linguistics as compared to the well-established tradition of historical linguistics, it is obvious that only a small part of the numerous problems involved in the description of a spoken language have been taken into account so far.

Paradoxically, Italian has received much more attention abroad than at home. Within the many possible fields of research, it is worth noting that Italian has received a first-choice treatment by non-Italian linguists, and almost every current descriptive theory has been applied to Italian. The contributions of, among others, North Americans, Germans, and Yugoslavs have been invaluable, and it is significant that most of the more useful tools in Italian linguistics have been written by foreign scholars (see Rohlfs 1949-54; Hall 1948, 1958a, 1971a; Muljačić 1969, 1971a; Tekavčić 1972a, 1972b, 1972c).

In more recent times, along with a wider spreading of current linguistic theories, interests in the native language have arisen in Italy, too, and research is rapidly increasing (making up, as it were, for lost time).

Of course, there are still many gaps in the field, and apart from any value judgments on the methods adopted, we sometimes have to quote an item only because it is the only one, not necessarily the best, on a certain topic. In many subfields we are not yet afforded a choice.

But, on the whole, the present state of the art seems a very promising one, and we can safely hope that from the melting pot of so many approaches and methodologies something valuable will surface in the immediate future. Meanwhile, the current atmosphere of scientific game-playing is extremely stimulating, and the feeling of a possible discovery at every step is precisely what makes linguistics an extremely exciting field today.

Many other important facets of linguistic research have been developed only recently in Italy: to quote only two examples, psycholinguistics and sociolinguistics. With those two approaches methodological interest is complemented by field work, and the feeling of having a grip on reality adds more practical interest. In our survey we have also included the developments occurring in these specialized fields.

I. GENERALITIES ON STANDARD ITALIAN

1.1 DEFINITION

The term *Standard Italian* is a somewhat fictitious label, aiming to circumscribe a hopelessly vague concept. As a matter of fact, in Italy there are at least four different possible levels of communication, each using a rather distinct linguistic code:

(a) a purely dialectal level	(e.g. Sardinian, or Piedmontese)
(b) dialectal Italian	(still a dialect, essentially, but with deep blendings of Italian morphological and lexical elements)
(c) regional Italian	(conversely, essentially Italian, but with many dialectal features, chiefly phonological and lexical ones)
(d) common Italian	(very roughly defined, a variety which has no peculiar regional features, unless minimal)

(for more details, see Berruto 1971, Cortelazzo 1972).

The most difficult to define is level (d). Maybe, in its written variety, it overlaps with the official written language, the language of the press and so on. But, as for the spoken variety, when, where, by whom, and to whom is common Italian spoken?

Let us assume that this common Italian will be called in what follows, *Standard Italian*, without any further qualification.

Historically, the core of Standard Italian is to be traced to the Tuscan-Florentine variety, a variety which has always had a very high standing in Italy, at least since the 14th century; among other reasons, it was used in their writings by such well-known authors as Dante, Petrarch, and Boccaccio. With the unification of Italy in 1870, this variety, which was already felt even by many non-Tuscans to be the "national language" (see the bibliography quoted under *2.1* and Bronzini

1971), became in effect the official language of Italy. In the last century, Italian underwent a number of adjustments, chiefly in phonology and lexicon, in view of its spreading over so many dialectal areas. But, on the whole, it has remained very conservative, at least from the point of view of its inner structure.

Owing to its recent spreading and to the fact that it is the mother tongue of only a minority of Italians, Standard Italian is by no means uniform throughout the country.

Luckily, our present aim is not to describe this variety, but to survey the studies which describe it, and since it is by far easier to discriminate between two descriptions of different varieties than between the two actual varieties, there shall be no doubt as to which item is to be considered in our survey, and which one not. Also the label *Standard Italian* is current in literature (see, e.g. the titles of Romeo 1966, Court 1967, Boström 1972); others use just *Italian*, without further qualifications, adding perhaps *Modern* or *Contemporary*, of course as opposed to *Ancient* or *Old*; see Bortolini - Tagliavini - Zampolli (1972), Karulin (1960), Savić (1965b), Widłak (1970).

Occasionally, other qualifications are also used: *Cultivated* (Rice 1946), and, when the emphasis is laid on written usage, *Literary* (German *italienische Schriftsprache*, Serbo-Croatian *književni jezik*, etc.).

As a more neutral label, the term *Standard Italian* seems to be the most suitable.

1.2 THE TYPOLOGY OF STANDARD ITALIAN

In an essay appended to the Italian translation of Bally's *Linguistique générale et linguistique française* C. Segre had to state that an analysis of Italian along the same lines as Bally's was still missing. He pointed out, quite relevantly:

> Le ragioni sono principalmente: la tradizione storicistica dei nostri studi, e la mancanza di una lingua parlata quotidiana abbastanza uniforme. Si tratta di fatti concomitanti: la labilità delle nostre strutture linguistiche, fratte nello spazio dal particolarismo dialettale, che influenza ancora potentemente anche la lingua, nel tempo dalla coesistenza di parole e forme appartenenti a diversi strati cronologici, da un lato rende periglioso ogni tentativo di ossificazione descrittiva, dall'altro invita ad una rassegna inevitabilmente diacronica degli elementi lessicali e grammaticali (Segre 1963b: 439).

The only, and at that, brief, examples of typological sketches, with typology of course used in a different sense than today, are Bartoli (1936), Wartburg (1936), Santoli (1942), Lewy (1942-43: 39-41), Lausberg (1947). Bartoli points out the place of Italian among Romance languages, and so does Wartburg; Santoli, Wartburg, and Lausberg outline a very brief comparison between Italian and - respectively - German, French, and Spanish, based on more obvious traits of either language.

Apart from Santoli's brief essay, all of them are very similar in that they consider chiefly the development of Italian from Latin as compared to the development of the other Romance languages: the relevant features of Italian are not considered as such, but with regard to differences in the other languages, as they developed from the same starting point. This approach is by no means to be criticized: the specific development of a language, provided that a starting point is given, is also a factor to be accounted for in its overall typological pattern. But of course, a typological description ought not to stop at this point.

The brief essay of Segre comes close to meeting the present requisites of typological analysis, and, even in the desultory fashion in which it is presented, it is an attempt to provide a third pole to Bally's French-German comparison, taking modern spoken Italian as its starting point. Most unfortunately, nothing more has been done since then from this point of view, and the more sophisticated methods of description presently at hand have not yet been employed in this connection. For a typology-oriented classification of Italian within Romance, see Contreras (1962-63) and Pellegrini (1970), quoted in the section below.

1.3 THE PLACE OF STANDARD ITALIAN IN ROMANCE

Almost every current handbook of Romance linguistics (Lausberg 1956, Vidos 1959, etc.; for an extensive sampling, see Pellegrini 1970) classifies as *Italian* one unit, adding Sardinian, and possibly Rhaeto-Romance and Ladin as separate units. This oversimplification has been strongly criticized. If one considers as separate "languages" only national languages, endowed with an ancient and well-established tradition, the inclusion of a Sardinian or a Ladin language could hardly be justified. We cannot speak of a "Sardinian" or of a "Ladin" language properly, since there does not exist a common form of Sardinian or Ladin on a par with, say, Spanish or French. But if we are to account for dialects, too, we are scarcely entitled to collect so many different linguistic entities as the dialects actually spoken in Italy under a single label *Italian*. Here again the distinction between "language" and "dialect" is likely to be misleading, unless we make a strong attempt toward a precise definition of the terms.

A more balanced classification is outlined by Monteverdi (1952: 80), who divides the whole Romance group in four large spaces or domains ("grandi spazi, o dominii"): Daco-Illyrian Romance, Italo-Romance, Gallo-Romance, and Ibero-Romance. Every domain groups two or more different units; in Italo-Romance there are Ladin, Upper Italian (namely, the dialects of Northern Italy), Italian, and Sardinian.

A similar device is adopted by Tagliavini (1972), whose Italo-Romance includes Dalmatian, Italian, Sardinian, Ladin. But, as Pellegrini (1970) rightly points out, an analogous independence is to be allotted to Southern Italian dialects, too. The best way of handling Romance classification is to determine the peculiar features, even of those units which traditionally are not accounted for. Making use of about forty "relevant features" (e.g. [± nasal vowels], [± stress] and so on), Muljačić (1967) and then Pellegrini (1970) have established a kind of matrix of a large number of units in Romance. Pellegrini has slightly improved Muljačić's inventory of relevant features, and, more significantly, has changed the point of view, choosing a different range of Romance languages. According to his analysis, Sardinian proves to be the most isolated language in the whole of Romance, and maybe this is not too new a piece of evidence. But it is worth recording that the second most isolated language is Lucanian, a completely neglected Southern Italian dialect. Then follow Roumanian, French, Portuguese, Italian (Tuscan), Vegliotic, Franco-Provençal, Spanish, Engadinese, Provençal, Frioulan, Catalan, Fassan, Cadorin. More striking differences would probably result from taking into account even more varieties of Italian (like Roumagnol, etc.).

II. HISTORY AND DEVELOPMENT

2.1 HISTORY OF THE LANGUAGE

There are abundant general surveys of the history of Italian language, but of course they are very uneven in value: we can quote Rohlfs (1937), Bertoni (1940), Pei (1941), Pulgram (1958), Schiaffini (1961), Grassi (1965a), ranging from a conference-size sketch (Schiaffini) to a general statement of the linguistic situation in Italy (Pulgram, Bertoni) from the very beginnings.

It is beyond the scope of this volume to survey special works dedicated to one or another period of Italian. But one exception ought to be made for the "questione della lingua", a heated debate concerning the variety of Italian to be adopted as the "Italian language", to which almost every major Italian writer and scholar has contributed at least once: there is a long series of contributions to the history of the "questione", and, to mention only volume-sized monographs, we can quote Labande-Jeanroy (1925), Hall (1942), Sozzi (1955), Vitale (1960). To these we can add a reprint of the papers of G.I. Ascoli on the "questione", edited and prefaced by C. Grassi (Ascoli 1967); the papers date back to the 1880's.

On the rise of Italian prose language we have an important paper by Kristeller (1946) and a book by Griffith (1967). Many collections of essays of single authors cover the history of the language, entirely or partially: see Parlangèli (1960), Segre (1963a).

The overall development of the Italian language is treated in two extremely different and therefore complementary works, Migliorini (1960) and Devoto (1953).

Migliorini (1960) is a compact and well-documented survey of the history of Italian from the Vulgar Latin period to 1915. The author sums up the results of his deep familiarity with the texts and problems of the Italian language and accordingly the book is more a *journal de voyage* of a life-long intimacy than a history of the development of Italian. The focus is chiefly on lexical aspects, orthography, grammatical debates; no attention is paid, for instance, to the development of syntax — on a purely linguistic plane — or to external sociolinguistic factors.

In a second edition of Migliorini (1960), a chapter by I. Baldelli is appended, in order to extend the history to the present day (Migliorini - Baldelli 1964; cf. Baldelli 1963); Migliorini's text has been translated into English and somewhat abri‹ by T.G. Griffith (Migliorini - Griffith 1966), who has also written an extra chapt‹ for the period after 1915: this edition, recast in view of the different audience, ‹ received well-deserved acclaim from reviewers ("one of the best modern historie: of a great standard language"; Hall 1967a: 977).

The much shorter book by Devoto (1953) is an extremely personal outline ("p filo") of the main trends of the literary language; as a reviewer has ingeniously pointed out, the design of the work resembles a network whose nodes are the crucial moments and characters (men, events, and works) chosen to represent their age. Emphasis is placed on historical events, rightly considered by the author as the pivots on which any cultural history has to move (see now Devoto 19

A simplified version of this outline − conceived for a broader audience − has been incorporated in Devoto - Altieri (1968), to which M.L. Altieri has contributed a substantial survey of more recent, literary as well as technical, developments of the language (pp. 129-323).

The recent essay by A. Stussi (1972) revolves essentially around the bipo- larity of standard language versus dialects in literature, from its origins to the present. The treatment is necessarily hasty, but nonetheless it is spiced with original assessments.

De Mauro (1963) is devoted to the history of the past century. The book is very awkwardly organized (the main bulk of the work consists of notes and appendices which are never integrated into the text): as it stands, it "gives the impression of having been put together in haste, perhaps (as is often the case in Italy) for an academic competition" (Hall 1964a: 95). The treatment is very desultory and belletristic, indulging in often utterly useless quotations of every imaginable kind. One could question, for instance, the reasons for quoting, second-hand, such an uncommon authority as the Christian Syriac writer of the 2nd century, Bardesanes, especially as this is done in support of a point quite contrary to the one made in the original text (De Mauro 1963: 12).

A good opportunity to recast the whole mass of the book in a more reliable and sophisticated fashion was lost in the second edition (1970). It offers no substantial improvements, and the accessory material tends to snowball, suf- focating the main text. Of course, the quotations have also been increased in number, and now the book opens with Vico, Wittgenstein, and Brecht, and closes with Goethe, much in the vein of Dalliac and Harbottle's *Dictionary of quotations.*

2.2 PRESENT TRENDS

Following critically the developments of a living language is a delicate task.
It requires the linguist's ability to discern the main trends among countless
facts and minor details. Again, we are still waiting for a proper history of
the past century; so far only scattered contributions have been given on certain aspects of this time span: see Devoto - Migliorini - Schiaffini (1962),
Baldelli (1963), De Mauro (1963).

The problems of modern language (correctness, peculiar features to be
avoided, etymology of new words, and so on) are obviously a very popular
topic among the average learned person. To meet such candid interest, many
linguists and philologists have been contributing popularized articles and lec-
tures to newspapers, magazines, and the mass media. Many of those texts,
couched in simple style, but sometimes scientifically accurate, have been collected in separate volumes; see for instance: Pasquali (1953), partially reprinted
in the larger Pasquali (1964); Peruzzi (1962, 1964), Migliorini (1962, 1968),
Menarini (1947, 1951), Tagliavini (1963).

But the problem with modern language in Italy is at a deeper level, beneath
surface oddities and quaintness. A proof of the depth of the problems is provided by a lively debate which arose in the years 1964-1967 on a new "questione della lingua". For perhaps the first time, the debate first arose among
laymen: writers, essayists, journalists, and all kinds of people interested in using the language, not in describing it (one of the contributors was P.P. Paso-
lini). Since the contributors were not linguists (who expect, when disputing,
to know exactly whatever the other is going to say, even before he speaks),
the debate was by far more interesting than an academic dispute. The main
topics were the relationships among the national language and the dialects,
the use of the dialects in literature and so on, and papers appeared scattered
in newspapers and magazines. The texts relevant to this debate have been
collected by Parlangèli (1971), who appropriately labeled the volume "La
nuova questione della lingua".

Seemingly, the problems raised have never been settled satisfactorily, and the
debate faded away for lack of fuel.

Insofar as description is concerned, a few analyses have been carried out on
the language of single authors, but since those works strive to pinpoint the
characteristics of a unique phenomenon (the "style" of the author), they seem
to pertain to another realm of interest, and they can scarcely be assumed to
represent a real portion of the modern standard language.

Special phenomena of the modern spoken language are treated regularly in
the Florentine quarterly *Lingua nostra*, which is the best mirror of the evolution
of syntax and lexicon in modern Italian today. For specimens of this attention

to shifts in contemporary usage, see Medici (1951, 1953), Migliorini (1952), D'Aronco (1952a, 1952b), Fochi (1953), Chiappelli (1954), Folena (1958), to quote just a few somewhat older examples.

A more systematic study of innovatory trends in the lexicon has been carried out by Junker (1955, 1958), Wandruszka (1958), Lintner (1962). Less work has been done on developments in the syntax: see Puccioni (1960), Nef-Reiner (1962), and Dardano (1968, 1969b, 1973a, 1973b), the last three contributions chiefly concerned with the language of newspapers.

III. PHONOLOGY

3.1 ARTICULATORY PHONETICS

It is hardly possible to survey research on the phonetics of Italian without quoting, from the very outset, the name of Amerindo Camilli.

Reflections and speculations about the phonetics of Italian are obviously traceable to a very remote time. In the 16th century, grammarians as well as writers (for instance, Trissino and Tolomei) devoted much effort to describing the sounds of Italian as accurately as possible; and some of them went so far as to elaborate a more accurate orthographic system, devising special signs in order to distinguish between /e/ and /ɛ/, /o/ and /ɔ/, etc. (see Migliorini 1960, passim).

But apart from those worthwhile attempts, the scientific description of Italian sounds is a very recent achievement, and it is to be credited to Camilli. Since the first decade of this century (his first valuable contribution is Camilli 1909) until his death (he was born in 1879 and died in 1960), Camilli wrote notes and articles on almost every aspect of Italian phonetics and orthography.

His methods were simple, as regards the level of sophistication, but they were by no means trivial, especially when taking into account the scientific background of Italian linguistics at the beginning of the century.

Camilli was a descriptivist in the best sense of the word. His contributions are always based on first-hand observations of the spoken language, collected and elaborated with a well-trained ear (Camilli was acquainted with the methods and findings of the best practical-phonetics schools of his days, as the British school of D. Jones).

In spite of his background, usually not favourably inclined to "foreign novelties" (as one derogatorily labeled any scientific method not devised in Italy) and to scientific biases in such an "idealistic" matter as language, he was sensible enough to capture the relevance of the then growing phonetic science and to keep himself up-to-date with rapidly developing British methods. So he devised an accurate Italian terminology to match the English one, and this terminology is still used in Italian today, whereas the cumbersome and often inaccurate terminology of his contemporaries is now completely outdated. He adopted wholeheartedly the basic principles of the International Phonetic Association (he co-authored, with D. Jones, the Italian version of the *Principles of IPA*, see Jones - Camilli 1933, and contributed steadily to *Le Maître phonétique*) and beyond any doubt he contributed more than anyone else to the scientific knowledge of Italian abroad (cf. Camilli 1921). A last point we would like to make, in order to indicate the scientific sensibility of this scholar: quite independently from any descriptivist school, he was deeply convinced of the relevance of current usage as against the bookish norms, and notwithstanding the prevailing trend, he gave recognition to different varieties of Italian besides Florentine (cf. Camilli 1938 for a brief description of the Roman variety).

Accordingly, his statements are almost free of any puristic bias towards the uniqueness of the Florentine variety. In order to appraise adequately such a realistic point of view, one has to recall that the Florentine variety used to be called the "Italian without adjectives", that is the only variety which could be called *Italian* without any further qualification and that also in very recent work on descriptive phonetics there is mention of a "correct" pronunciation (the Florentine one) versus a "wrong" one (the remaining ones: see Fiorelli 1964, Tagliavini 1965; against this position see the remarks of Lepschy 1966).

In the final bibliography of the present volume a choice of Camilli's items is listed. A posthumous edition of Camilli (1941a), very carefully edited by P. Fiorelli in 1965, includes a large selection of materials (published minor notes, manuscript corrections) which represents the final summary of the author's opinions on a number of points.

In describing Italian phonetics, if one dismisses the very important question of which variety is to be described, and assumes that this variety is the cultivated Florentine one, fuzzy points are not so many, and they are chiefly the points not accounted for by the orthography. One has only to argue that this onesided assumption was made too often and that we know too little about the other varieties of Italian.

One of the first important contributions was Camilli (1909 = 1965: 9-10) which recognized three different degrees in Italian consonants (lax, medium, and tense); Davis (1937) recognized more degrees of openness in vowels than the usual two [o]: [ɔ] and [e] : [ɛ], but his findings are questioned by Castellani (1956).

A brief survey of articulatory phonetics, merged with a phonemic statement, is to be found in Hall (1948: 7-17); much more detailed are Castellani (1956) and Fiorelli (1952).

Some of the work in Italian phonetics had a practical purpose, too, namely the definition of a standard norm of reference. Much on those lines is the work on orthography, aiming to suggest improvements on traditional spelling in order to avoid doubts and fluctuations: see for instance Migliorini (1941c), Malagòli (1939, 1941), Camilli (1941b, 1953a), Castellani (1962a).

An important reference book from the point of view of establishing a normative standard in pronunciation (and, to a lesser extent, in spelling) is Bertoni - Ugolini (1939b). Here for the first time a new normative concept is employed, that of the 'Rome-Florence axis' ("l'asse Roma-Firenze"), put forth in Bertoni - Ugolini (1939a). In giving recognition to Roman usage in the constitution of a standard pronunciation, the coauthors were aiming to balance the traditional linguistic relevance of Florence with the growing political influence of the capital, Rome.

Of course, this simple device aiming to have it both ways, to recognize the sociolinguistic status of Florence without diminishing the importance of Rome, today seems completely devoid of linguistic justification. One could hardly conceive why, if the criterium of a unique focal area is abandoned, only another local usage is to be taken into account as a source of correctness; why only Rome, and not, for instance, Milan, just to have another part of Italy represented? The only possible explanation lies in the lip service paid – in the thirties – to Rome, the ideal focus of the painfully built cult of Latin and Roman civilization favored by Fascism.

In more recent times, when the tribute to Rome was no longer necessary, normativists have completely rehabilitated Florentine pronunciation as the only possible model. The most recent example of this trend is to be seen in the *Dizionario di ortografia e di pronunzia* (Migliorini - Tagliavini - Fiorelli 1969), which gives only the Florentine pronunciation for every entry, even when Roman forms are more in accordance with the usual Standard Italian development of Latin sounds.

We are very poorly informed about regional variants of pronunciation of Italian; see Camilli (1938) for Rome, Quaresima (1962) for Trient, Leone (1954) for Sicily, Castellani (1956) and Fiorelli (1952) for vernacular Florentine, Clivio (1970) for Piedmont; much information is scattered through Tagliavini (1965), even if the variants are listed more as mistakes to be corrected than as legitimate local pronunciations.

But a proper phonetic atlas of regional Italian is still lacking.

3.2 INSTRUMENTAL PHONETICS

Instrumental phonetics — P. Meriggi was able to state in 1930 — began very early, almost with its first steps, to deal with Italian ("La fonetica sperimentale incominciò assai di buon'ora, fin quasi dai suoi primi passi, ad occuparsi dell'italiano"; Meriggi 1930: 211). The first instrumental account of Italian phonetics dates from the end of the 19th century and the beginnings of the 20th (Josselyn 1899a, 1899b, 1901, 1904), that is just a few years after the beginning of Rousselot's experimental research.

Josselyn's work, which is still useful to a certain extent, gave rise to a long series of research. Goidànich's critique (Goidànich 1910) is not too important. It concerns the articulatory characters of [tš, ts, dž], which he labels "rattratte" ('contracted'), but it added nothing to Josselyn's findings (for both authors they are simple and not compound sounds); but the research of G. Panconcelli - Calzia, an Italian-born scholar who worked in Hamburg, was very important and stimulating. Panconcelli - Calzia carried on experiments on consonants, pitch and intonation of Italian, and published a brief survey of Italian phonetics based entirely on instrumental evidence (Panconcelli - Calzia 1911).

P. Meriggi, another Italian scholar, trained by Panconcelli - Calzia, published some reports on his own work (Meriggi 1928, on expiratory intensity; Meriggi 1929, on plosives) and a careful survey of previous work in the field (Meriggi 1930). In a few years, Meriggi was to give up phonetic studies (even if not entirely) and to become one of the best-known specialists in Ancient Near Eastern languages. With Meriggi's articles ends a brief but very lively tradition of studies in Italian phonetics, and contributions tend to be more and more scattered through the years. We can quote useful papers by Parmenter - Treviño (1930) on pitch, Parmenter - Carman (1932) on vowel length, and Richter (1940) on the nature of [š, tšj]. Gemelli - Pastori (1934), a fundamental step in instrumental analysis, is more method-oriented than language-oriented, and gives but scarce information of linguistic value, even if most of its examples are drawn from Italian.

On the whole, those analyses were too isolated to be really useful, and sometimes mechanical devices were employed without a specific background to support them. A case in point is an article by R. Giacomelli (1954), in which the author tries to ascertain differences between pronunciations of /-tš-/ and /-š-/ availing himself of a kymograph (ignoring the fact that, since a distinction in the place of articulation was involved, this device was utterly useless, and that an artificial palate would do much better).

The rapidly improving quality of instrumental analysis nowadays requires an ever deeper level of analysis and also an impressive array of machinery and devices (sound spectrographs, pitch meters, cine-radiology equipment, breath pressure and flow transducers, and so on) which unfortunately are too hard to assemble in a single laboratory. On the other hand, phonological analysis in its most sophisticated versions requires more and more knowledge of the purely *phonetic* correlates of classificatory features.

That means that a deeper and surer knowledge of Italian phonetics, which cannot be reached today except with instrumental methods, is also a strong prerequisite for a better phonological analysis.

Evidence emerging from the new trend in instrumental phonetics gives very interesting results. For instance, Rosenzweig (1965) found, on the basis of spectrographic analysis, that consonantal length is a more consistently recurring feature than vocalic length (and Di Pietro 1971: 720 reports evidence of his own, supporting Rosenzweig's findings); this piece of evidence seems to settle the choice between the two possible solutions: phonemically long vowels and automatically short consonants or phonemically long consonants and automatically short vowels, with vowels in stressed position (/pa:la/ [pa:la] 'shovel' : /pala/ [pal:a] 'ball', or /pala/ [pa:la] : /pal:a/ [pal:a] ?).

Good hopes for regular research on instrumental analysis could be fostered in view of the recent establishment of an acoustic laboratory sponsored by the University of Padua and the Italian National Research Council, which promises a spectrographic atlas of Italian articulatory types: the first results of a series of spectrographic analyses have begun to be published: see Magno Caldognetto - Abati - Dossi (1971a, 1971b), Croatto *et alii* (1971), Magno Caldognetto (1971), Magno Caldognetto - Fava (1974).

Particularly relevant is Magno Caldognetto (1971), which gives phonetic correlates of compact/diffuse and grave/acute features for /p, t, k/.

An accurate analysis of Italian vowels has been carried out by E.F. Ferrero (1968, 1972; Ferrero - Stalhammer 1972), as a specimen of broader research in progress, sponsored by the Istituto Elettrotecnico Nazionale "Galileo Ferraris" of Turin.

3.3 AUTONOMOUS PHONEMICS

The first phonemic analysis of Italian (taking the term in its narrower sense) was attempted by Porru (1939). Even if subsequent research has severely criticized Porru's analysis, in view of its inadequate treatment of the evidence, it remains that this was one of the first phonemic analyses of a European language to be carried out along the lines of Prague phonology. An important critical article on Porru was written by Malmberg (1942-43).

A more accurate phonemicization of Italian was produced in 1944 by R.A.

Hall, Jr. Hall (1944) assigns 27 phonemes to Italian (Porru assigned it 42-44), and, with slight modifications, the same holds true also for the first edition of Hall's Italian grammar (Hall 1948). Even within a taxonomic framework of analysis, subsequent explications were most uneven: taking the overall number of phonemes assigned in every description as a term of comparison, we have, as opposed to the 27 phonemes assumed by Hall, 43 for Lausberg (1947), 50 for Fiorelli (1952, 1964), 50-53 for Castellani (1956), 50 for Busa *et alii* (1963), 44-46 for Franceschi (1964) (there is a useful chart of different proposed analyses in Muljačić 1969: 440-1). Such a striking fluctuation deserves a short comment. Many differences are due to the interpretation of geminates: many authors assign simple and geminate sounds to different phonemes (for instance in *calo* 'diminution' : *callo* 'corn', *caro* 'dear' : *carro* 'cart', etc.). Since almost all consonantic sounds can occur in simple as well as in geminate form in Italian, that means assigning almost twice the number of consonants to the final description. But other differences are due to the type of Italian analyzed. For instance, one controversy in the descriptions of Italian is the treatment of [-z-]. Some consider it a separate phoneme /z/, and others an intervocalic allophone of /s/ ([z-] does not occur in Italian except before voiced consonants). But only in certain varieties (e.g. in Florentine) does such minimal pair as *fuso* [fuzo] 'melted' and *fuso* [fuso] 'spindle' exist; in those varieties we are perfectly entitled to assign [z] and [s] to two different phonemes. On the other hand, in many other varieties (including, by the way, the one the present writer speaks), only [-z-] occurs intervocalically, never [-s-] . For those speakers there is no reason to posit a ghost phoneme /z/. A similar situation holds also for /e, o/ vs. /ɛ,ɔ/, whose distribution is very uneven in different varieties of Italian (the majority of Italian speakers merge th four phonemes into two, /e/ and /o/).

It would seem sound procedure to account for these differences in descriptio But unfortunately most published analyses have ignored or dismissed geographical variety within Italian, and scholars have kept on searching for the most farfetched minimal pairs, as *isa!* ['isa] 'heave ho! ' and *Isa* ['iza] (feminine proper name), *taso* ['taso] 'tartar' and *Taso* ['tazo] 'Thasus', and so on (a full list of such phonological monsters has been collected by Muljačić 1969: 414-16).

The obstacle was removed by Hall (1960b), who assumed a "semicomponential analysis"; /e/, /o/, and /s/ can also have a phonological component, tenseness versus laxness for the two vowels, and voice versus non-voice for the sibilant: for instance *venti* ['venti] '20' and *venti* ['vɛnti] 'winds' are to be phonemicized as /ve^nti/ and /venti/ respectively, where the symbol /^/ indicates the occurrence of the tenseness component. This device permits a representation of different varieties, marking the opposition between /e/ and /ɛ/ only when it effectively holds true. Romeo (1966) took a stand against this solution, assuming there are separate phonemes; see the well-balanced rejoinder by Hall (1967b).

It is worth noting that such a well-developed battery of discovery procedures as the taxonomic technique, as it was elaborated chiefly by North American scholars, had left the field of Italian almost untouched, apart from the endeavor of Hall: as a matter of fact, a series of papers completing the taxonomic analysis of Italian is relatively recent: Krámský (1964), Lepschy (1964), Di Pietro (1965), Agard - Di Pietro (1965a), Romeo (1966, 1967, 1968); Garde (1968) on stress; Klajn (1967), Lichem (1969).

The most recent synthesis of this kind of analysis is the phonological chapter in Hall (1971a), which sums up the author's own findings in the autonomous phonology of Italian. For a survey of the state of the art Saltarelli (1970a) is also useful, and so to a larger extent is Muljačić (1969, 1972a).

Statistical elaborations of the Italian phonemic inventory have been carried on in Zipf - Rogers (1939), Busa *et alii* (1963), Krámský (1964), Zampolli (1968, 1973).

3.4 SYSTEMIC PHONEMICS

Even if much more recent than autonomous phonemics, the systemic approach has already yielded a mass of fruitful insights into our knowledge of Italian phonology.

The binaristic approach has been adopted by Muljačić, who proposed a full matrix of binary distinctive features of Italian (see Muljačić 1964, 1966, 1968, 1969, 1972a). Muljačić's attempt is a very interesting one, since the author has accomplished the most comprehensive survey of the problems involved in Italian phonology, up to date, and has attempted to account for regional varieties in his description. Of course, the inventory of features could be improved, chiefly on the basis of a better instrumental knowledge of phonetic correlates; see Di Pietro (1970), Scalise (1971), Magno Caldognetto (1971).

The binaristic approach is, at any rate, still far from being proper generative phonology, as it is expounded, for instance, in Chomsky and Halle's *The sound pattern of English* (Chomsky - Halle 1968), in that it limits itself to a description of segments in terms of relevant features, but does not make any generalization concerning the processes involved. Muljačić again has made a first attempt toward a better exploitation of his methods: in Muljačić (1971b) he tries to predict morphological phenomena in terms of binaristic phonology.

A purely generativist approach has been elaborated by Di Pietro (1967), Valesio (1971a) on sibilants, and Crisari (1969) on the phonemic status of [v], where diachronic problems are also involved; Costabile (1972) tries to predict,

18

within a generativist approach, the place of stress.

In his doctoral dissertation, completed in 1966 but published in 1970 (Saltarelli 1970a), M. Saltarelli tries to elaborate the first comprehensive application of standard generative phonology to Italian. His basic assumption is that vowel length plays a central role in Italian phonology. Accordingly, the vowel system turns out to have fourteen units: /e eː, i iː, o oː, u uː, ɛ ɛː, ɔ ɔː, a aː/.

It will be noted that Valesio (1967) had already suggested phonemically long vowels in Italian, in order to account for such minimal pairs as *dormii* [dorˈmiː] 'I slept' and *dormi* [dorˈmi] 'he slept', but he limited himself to /iː/ and /eː/. This assumption was required by the consideration of an underlying morphological level: in *ninféa* 'water-lily' versus *ninfée* 'water-lilies', the last *-e* is a plural marker; likewise, the second *-i* in *dormii, salii*, etc. is an inflectional marker.

But Saltarelli's assumption of a complete set of long vowels is certainly new, and overturns the more common view, according to which vowel length automatically complements consonantal tenseness. As for consonantic segments, Saltarelli's inventory is almost identical with the usual one: twenty consonants, with /ts/ and /dz/, but without /z/. For these 34 non-redundantly specified segments, eleven distinctive features are required. For a careful review of Saltarelli (1970a; Saltarelli 1970b presents the same set of evidence, but it is written in Italian, and in a more accessible fashion), see Di Pietro (1971b) and Scalise (1971).

It would seem that much work remains to be done in order to have an adequate treatment of Italian phonology, but many points seem to have been satisfactorily determined now.

Apart from some refinements in the general framework of the standard theory, it would be worthwhile to call upon a natural phonological approach, and in this trend Valesio's first attempt (Valesio 1971a) on the grammar of sibilants seems fully adequate.

Another major improvement would be to take regional varieties into account. An adequate framework could explain regional differences, and again Valesio's treatment seems to account satisfactorily for the distribution of [-s-] and [-z-] within the Italian area.

3.5 DIACHRONIC PHONOLOGY

The grounds for having a diachronic section separate from the treatment of autonomous and systemic analysis are that only in rare cases has the diachronic study of Italian phonology been molded into an overall phonological theory.

The time is not yet ripe for a mature synthesis. We need many more detailed descriptive studies like those of Castellani (1954, 1960, 1961-1965) on different cross-sections of diachronic Italian before attempting to suggest a solid explication of the sound development in Italian.

A great deal of scattered evidence is collected throughout Rohlfs (1949), with no explicative theory. Tekavčić (1972a) tries to cast these data in a Martinetian pattern. On the much discussed point of *e o s z* there is a short monograph by Franceschi (1965; for a negative review see Valesio 1967b). Lepschy (1965) reconstructs a phonemic contrast which lasted until the 16th century, and then merged. We can safely assume that the whole field is wide open to newer approaches, and much work remains to be done.

3.6 CONTRASTIVE ANALYSIS

The practice of contrastive analysis is on the whole quite recent, but there are already many good accounts for Italian compared to other languages.

Probably the first attempt is Arce (1962) for Italian and Spanish. A more developed treatment is Agard - Di Pietro (1965a), a companion volume of which is dedicated to grammar (1965b); Niculescu (1969) deals with Roumanian. A very interesting experiment, in view of the unusual situation accounted for, is Mioni (1971), which describes the phonological competence of a single speaker, multilingual in Kikuyu, Swahili, English, and Italian. Mioni has also written a practical handbook for the contrastive analysis of Italian, on the one hand, and eleven European languages on the other. A great deal of evidence is packed into little space; the author discusses in length previous treatments of the phonemics of each one of the languages concerned, adding many solutions of his own (Mioni 1973).

IV. GRAMMAR

4.0 THE TRADITIONAL BACKGROUND

Until very recent times, tradition in Italian grammar was on the whole very conservative. Up until 1948 (a turning point, in a sense, in view of the publication of Hall's grammar) a long series of sharply prescriptivist grammars (minutely surveyed by Hall (1958a) displayed the well-known Graeco-Latin pattern of description.

The older grammars (and sometimes the more recent ones, too) have these common features:

(a) Data are drawn from the whole gamut of Italian literature: the oldest writers are quoted side by side with modern ones, which means that a span of almost six centuries of Italian literature is covered.

(b) No indication is given of different levels of usage, sociolinguistic factors, geographical varieties, and so on: the kind of language presented – which is the Florentine variety of classical authors – is assumed to be a monolithic reality, the direct heir of Classical Latin (of course it is, but exactly as any other Romance variety) and the purest among all the offspring of Latin.

(c) Written and spoken language are confused; when spoken language is quoted, samples are drawn from the Florentine vernacular: in this way, certain regional features are privileged over other regional features, with no theoretically valid reasons.

(d) Grammatical categories are the traditional Graeco-Latin ones. There is no effort to make them agree with the actual shape of the Italian language: sometimes definitions are drawn from outside the language itself: typical for instance is the distinction between abstract and concrete nouns, which is supported only by a distinction among "things" on the one hand, and abstract "qualities", "actions" and so on, on the other.

But there is no point in pursuing such an inventory. We can find exactly the same kind of problems in every European grammatical tradition, and everywhere this type of grammatical tradition is traceable to at least the 16th century (for a survey of the history of Italian grammatical tradition see Trabalza 1908).

4.1 GENERAL STUDIES

It would be easy to draw up a long list of titles of Italian grammars; even if they are of little or no theoretical value, they are to be credited at least for a good choice of literary examples. Accordingly, they can be used as a store of grammatical data, more than as an explication of them.

The old handbook of Vockeradt (1878) is worth recording for the large space given to syntax; among the many grammars published at the end of the 19th century, Fornaciari (1879 and 1881) still remain useful; Petrocchi (1887) is too short, even as a reference book. An example of a grammar based on Florentine usage is Morandi - Cappuccini (1894), which describes the usage of cultivated people of Florence, asserting the supremacy of the Florentine variety for recently unified Italy. Italian linguists, preferring older states of the language, or dialects, have been rarely, if ever, tempted to write a grammar of their own language. True to this tradition, even G.I. Ascoli, the father − so to speak − of linguistics in Italy, who made many contributions to the study of a score of Indo-European and Semitic languages and of Italian dialects, never wrote on the Italian standard language, except for a very illuminating series of papers and pamphlets on the "questione della lingua" (see Ascoli 1967), a topic that in his day was more political than scientific. Grammar-writing was, accordingly, the business of philologists, historians of literature, teachers, amateurs. An exception to the rule was Goidànich, a scholar concerned with many fields of linguistic endeavour (for an assessment of his work see the preface by L. Heilmann to the 1962 edition of Goidànich 1918); among more recent works, Trabalza - Allodoli (1934), despite its rather ambitious title *La grammatica degli Italiani*, deserved the sharp criticism it received from reviewers (see for instance Schiaffini 1953: 145-54), in view of the confused methods adopted, tinged with idealistic and pseudophilosophical speculation. Representative of the intellectual climate of Italian studies throughout Fascism is the fact that examples have been expanded in order to make room for lenghthy enthusiastic quotations of B. Mussolini, along with Dante, Petrarch, and Manzoni. A still more recent grammar, Battaglia - Pernicone (1951), deserves some attention, but only for documentary materials. In more recent times, a host of grammars have been written also by reputed linguists, chiefly as secondary-school handbooks, but none of them seems to display any original trait; maybe, the only one worth noting is Migliorini (1941b).

4.2 HISTORICAL GRAMMAR

The first treatment of Italian from a historical point of view (in the vein of comparative philology prevailing in the eighties) is perhaps a short sketch by D'Ovidio and Meyer-Lübke, written for the *Grundriss der romanischen Philologie* (D'Ovidio - Meyer-Lübke 1888); phonetics and morphology are treated from a historical point of view, that is, traced to their Latin antecedent. Of course, in this frame of reference there would be but little space left for syntax, and in fact syntax was not treated at all. Two years later a comprehensive grammar of Italian was published by Meyer-Lübke (1890), and this was to become a standard work for comparative research (see also the two somewhat recast Italian editions: D'Ovidio - Meyer-Lübke 1906, Meyer-Lübke 1901). The design of this kind of grammar, in which the starting point was the list of phonological and morphological phenomena of Latin and the point of arrival the result of their modification in the course of time, became the obligatory frame of reference for every historical description, and it became usual to describe any linguistic evidence in Romance with reference to Latin and under Latin headings (not "The vowels of language *x* are such and such", but "the continuations of Latin $\breve{e}$ and $\bar{e}$ in language *x* are such and such").

This kind of presentation seems us today to atomize any systematicity underlying the language: the sounds of a language were described not in their own terms or according to their mutual relationships, but rather according to their relations to Latin sounds. It would seem impossible to have continued construing grammar in this way after the twenties; but apparently this view was too deeply rooted to be eliminated. In 1927 Grandgent produced a concise handbook of historical phonology and morphology (Grandgent 1927), and about twenty years after, G. Rohlfs published a monumental historical grammar of Italian (Rohlfs 1949) which, from a theoretical point of view, reproduced exactly the same frame found in Meyer-Lübke (1890; the only difference was the improvement in terms of linguistic refinement). Of course the bulk of data is enormously expanded in Rohlfs' work. More Italian texts were published in the meantime with better philological care, a broad linguistic atlas was completed, and the study of dialects was greatly improved. Rohlfs himself has an impressive first-hand knowledge of many dialectal areas of Italy, which he has surveyed extensively.

Availing himself of all these advancements in the state of the art, Rohlfs was able to collect a massive amount of data from almost every point in space and time in the history of Italian.

It is only acknowledging the obvious to point out the unique rank attained by Rohlfs' grammar among standard works on Italian. For almost every documentary problem, one can be sure to find there a reliable aid and plentiful evidence

But, as far as method, arrangement of data, and explicative adequacy are concerned, the work is more a catalogue of facts than a true grammar: no attempt is made to explain phenomena, and almost none of the achievements of modern descriptive linguistics has found its way into the text. Nor does the Italian translation, which the author himself checked and improved, show any sign of modernization.

Recently, steps have been taken to rewrite Rohlfs (1949) in accordance with tenets of modern linguistics by Tekavčić (1972); a structuralist approach, based chiefly on Pottier's and Alarcos Llorach's morphosyntax and Martinet's phonology, is adopted throughout (cf. chiefly Pottier 1958, Alarcos Llorach 1951, Martinet 1955). The main body of examples is drawn from Rohlfs, but important additions, chiefly from Vulgar Latin, are also added. The treatment is interesting, even if sometimes uneven: the sections on the lexicon are rather poor compared to the coverage of other parts; no treatment is given of stress and pitch; bibliographical references are not very up-to-date, and serious gaps occur, but on the whole Tekavčić has made a praiseworthy effort to give a diachronic perspective to the mass of data, and to explain some processes and mergings, with the aid of such graphic devices as tracings, schemes, and so on. Every form is handled within a valid framework, and it is possible to see structural relationships among forms of the same language and of different languages, which was hardly possible with Rohlfs. One of the most regrettable shortcomings of such an important and painstaking work is the complete oblivion of every kind of linguistics related to transformational grammar, which, whether we appreciate it or not, is here to stay. This attitude is mirrored in the scarce attention paid to syntax: Tekavčić is quite right in arguing that it is wrong to distinguish between the treatment of syntax and that of morphology (Tekavčić 1972b: 5) because they are "indissolubly bound"; but it seems equally wrong to dissolve syntax into a sprinkling of morphemes.

Also the coverage of single points is very unequal. Historical syntax, if we mean by this term the diachronic study of single syntactic patterns, is very superficially treated. As we shall see again and again, the lack of a suitable frame of reference in describing historical phenomena, apart from the purely Neogrammarian one, which is hardly to be defined as a theory, seriously hinders every work in this field. More fruitful are, at least at present, studies of certain cross-sections of older Italian; many monographs have been published on older Italian, and we shall quote Brambilla Ageno (1964) and Ambrosini (1960-61) on the verb, Dardano (1969a) on narrative prose syntax, Savić (1965b) on concessive constructions, and on tense usage in the *Decameron* (Savić 1962), Cernecca (1963, 1968) on various syntactic phenomena in literary language.

The genesis of the Romance future has been studied by Valesio (1968, 1969), who proposed an ingenious explication; morphological points have been discussed by Politzer (1952, 1958), Aebischer (1960, 1961), Sabatini (1965), Durante (1962), Brodin (1970), Boström (1972), and many others. A considerable amount of accurate data is collected in such works as Brodin (1970), but since important structural as well as semantic aspects have been left out, these collections serve only as a starting point for deeper-reaching research.

4.3 DESCRIPTIVE GRAMMAR

4.3.1 *Comprehensive descriptions*

In a sense, every grammarian should practice descriptive grammar, exactly as does that character in Molière who learns that he has been speaking prose all his life. In fact every earnest grammar of Italian ought to be at least descriptive, and surely the work of some of the previously quoted authors was descriptive. But if we construe the term *descriptive* in a narrower and more precise sense, the first attempt to give a full descriptive grammar of Italian is Hall (1948). This quite remarkable work was carried on within the framework of post-Bloomfieldian linguistics (Hall himself was Bloomfield's pupil and he acknowledges Bloomfield's aid and criticism among others, in a footnote). It displays all the major achievements of structuralist linguistics: the corpus is sharply cut off in time, native informants from different regions of Italy are used, with little or no resort to written sources; accordingly strict attention is paid to the spoken language, and this fact is underscored by the use of a phonemic transcription throughout the text; each category is accounted for in terms of forms and morphemes, and so on. The section devoted to syntax is very reduced, in accordance with the scant feeling for syntax of those days, but the chapter on derivation is exceptionally extended, and it merges in itself a good deal of traditional morphology. Hall (1948), seen from our present point of view, was certainly an extremely useful achievement in the history of Italian grammar, and certainly a starting point for further analysis. But unfortunately, the time was not ripe and the challenge was not accepted; in Italy, Hall's grammar had very little impact and did not help to improve the then current methodology of grammar-writing. A second thoroughly revised edition (Hall 1971a), written in Italian, adds substantial improvements, mainly in the treatment of syntax, to the nucleus of the first edition.

In more recent times many other descriptive grammars have been published; they are mostly intended for practical use, as reference books for students of Italian, in view of the scarcity of available materials, and are all the work of Italianists abroad: Manuppella (1952-53), Petkanov (1956), Hijmans Tromp

(1964), Regula - Jernej (1965), Brunet (1971), Fogarasi (1969), Herczeg (1970). Owing to the prevailing pedagogical concerns, the method adopted by those authors is a moderated version of structuralism, smoothed out where too apparent a contrast could arise with more conventional descriptions. For instance, the somewhat rigid descriptivist criterion of Hall, according to whom a bound form like /som/ or /em/ or /stom/, which occur only in scientific words like *somatico*, *ematico*, *stomatite*, etc. is to be considered an Italian form with a meaning of its own, is, in view of its distributional properties, not adopted by other linguists.

As for other available grammars, Guryčeva (1966) is just a very short outline of the main grammatical features, despite the rather ambitious title (*Comparative and contrastive grammar of the Romance languages. Italo-Romance subgroup*). Agard - Di Pietro (1965b) encompasses a structural description of Italian morphology and of the main sentence types in an interesting essay on the contrastive analysis of the chief grammatical structures of English and Italian.

Perhaps one of the best among the moderate structuralist treatments of Italian is Fogarasi's grammar (Fogarasi 1969): the method chosen by the author is allegedly somewhat between "le rigorose esigenze metodologiche di A. Martinet" and traditional grammar. But in spite of this anything but revolutionary choice, the work features many interesting aspects: the treatment of intonation (Fogarasi 1969: 59-72), supported by intonation-contour drawings, is useful and completely new. The chapter on the lexicon is well elaborated and up-to-date; use is made of Alinei (1962), and accordingly morpheme frequencies are utilized; real spoken language is also quoted, and many a typically spoken construction, which one would search in vain in other grammars, is to be found in Fogarasi.

4.3.2 Research on individual topics

4.3.2.1 Morphology

The study of morphology is the one in which shortcomings in descriptive methods are least apparent. Possible arrangements of morphemes, and the morphemes themselves, appear to the analyst with an impressive self-evidence. This is one of the reasons which account for the high number of papers on various aspects of Italian morphology, beginning with Reinhardstöttner (1871), Barmeyer (1886), and Goidànich (1893).

For a choice of papers in which the traditional methods of historical grammar are applied, we can quote Consiglio (1946), Migliorini (1949), Heinimann (1949), Leone (1957), Medici (1959), Bonfante (1961, 1964), Migliorini (1964), Moffa (1964), and Leone (1966). A rigid descriptivist method is displayed in a long series of papers by Hall (1956, 1958b, 1959, 1960a, 1960b, 1964b); a somewhat different, softer framework is used by Giurescu (1967), Tekavčić (1968a, 1968b), and Durante (1970).

4.3.2.2 Syntax

For reasons complementary to those quoted above, the study of Italian syntax, even along traditional lines, is more recent and, if we were to judge from bibliographical references, it is also that which Italian scholars are least interested in. A series of brief papers was published in *Italica* (Vaughan 1926) and *Lingua nostra* (Devoto 1940; Ronconi 1942, 1943, 1944-55; Růžička 1943). Devoto (1940) deals with a topic that is hardly ever touched in traditional grammar, the "aspect" of the Italian verb (e.g. *lavoro* versus *sto lavorando*), which has only recently been revised: Musa (1970), Saronne (1970), Cîrstea (1972), Lucchesi (1972). The number of articles and monographs devoted to syntax is increasing very rapidly: Nilsson - Ehle (1947), Sorrento (1950), Strohmeyer (1950), Huber-Sauter (1951), Guţia (1953), Mortara (1956), Mourin (1956), Guţia (1958), Karulin (1960), Jernej (1961), Savić (1962), Cernecca (1962), Skubic (1965), Savič (1966), Kässmayer-Beran (1965) Skubic (1966-68, 1967), Alisova (1967), Jernej (1967).

Herczeg has written a long series of papers and books on various sentence types and on the use of different tenses (Herczeg 1954, 1955, 1957, 1959a, 1959b, 1962a, 1962b, 1963a, 1963b, 1964, 1965, 1966, 1967, 1969, 1972b).

All these contributions move along very similar lines: the terminology and methodological framework is − on the whole − traditional, but each author strives to collect a rich exemplification on his chosen topics. The usefulness of these papers lies, first of all, in the vast amount of data drawn from spoken, but more often written (and literary), sources; in this way it is possible to find constructions which traditional reference grammars often completely dismiss.

This patient spadework of arrangement and systematicization, even if it does not give any relevant insight into the deep structure of sentences, provides a reliable basis for further research. Furthermore, even if the semantic component of the syntax is not treated as such, authors often have a stylistic interest in the use of certain constructions: in G. Herczeg's work this interest is quite apparent, and it helps the author to state many insights into the meaning of certain constructions, even if not in a systematic way.

An attempt at a systematic explicative description of the verbal system in Italian is Tekavčić (1970a), which establishes functional binary oppositions of verbal categories, in accordance with Alarcos Llorach's *Gramática estructural* (Alarcos Llorach 1951). An analogous attempt has been made by Lo

Cascio (1968) for a portion of the verbal system, but on the whole such functional explanations are somewhat rare. See also Schmitt-Jensen (1970), a lengthy analysis of the usage of the subjunctive mood.

Particular emphasis has been laid on the function of word order in Italian: see Jernej (1967), Sciarone (1969, 1970), Cernecca (1972), Muljačić (1972b); but the taxonomic methods seem to have yielded all they can, and it is high time for research to begin to account for something else besides surface structure.

4.4 TRANSFORMATIONAL-GENERATIVE GRAMMAR

4.4.0 *Generalities*

Tranformational-generative grammar has affected the analysis of Italian in a very limited way, and the Chomskyan revolution has penetrated perhaps too late into the domain of Italian linguistics.

Typically, almost all the generative analyses of Italian have been carried out by non-Italians, or by Italians working abroad: Alinei (1966), Schwarze (1967), Krenn (1970, 1971, 1972), Puglielli (1968), Swanson (1968), Giurescu (1972), Seuren (1971), Clivio (1972), and Ebneter (1972). In Italy, transformational grammar has not caught on, especially in academic circles, and it is beyond the scope of the present survey to inquire into the reasons for this utter refusal. We can just add that no realistic debate has been raised in Italy on the subject, and the Chomskyan approach has never been discussed with good knowledge of the case by its opponents.

Nonetheless, in very recent times a trend toward transformational grammar has developed in Italy. Papers on these topics appear regularly in *Lingua e stile, Studi italiani di linguistica teorica e applicata*, and in the proceedings of the Società Italiana di Linguistica, and it has been possible to dedicate a whole conference of the latter society (*Atti* 1971a) to this kind of approach.

4.4.1 *Standard theory*

Among the first attempts toward a transformational-generative framework in Italian, we must quote Alinei (1966), Krenn (1967), Schwarze (1967), Puglielli (1967), and Costabile (1967). Costabile is at the same time an attempt at a comprehensive transformational-generative grammar of Italian; the work was carried out along the lines of Chomsky's *Aspects* (Chomsky 1965), but the explicative power of the treatment is very weak. Sometimes we are confronted with mere rewriting rules, which give no real insight into the "structures of

Italian". One of the points misconstrued by the author is that an adequate grammatical theory has not only to predict all the possible grammatical sentences, but also to rule out impossible sentences. Another point that deserves criticism is the overwhelming number of rules called for, which seems to point to an inadequate depth of the analysis level.

None else has ever attempted an overall treatment of Italian, but Puglielli (1967, 1969, 1970) is tantamount to a minimal grammar, in accordance with standard theory. Large fragments of a generative grammar of Italian are included in Antinucci (1970), Lo Cascio (1969, 1970), Colombo (1971), and Alisova (1972), whose theoretical framework overlaps only partially with the standard theory.

For the sake of brevity, we can quote two volumes of proceedings, *Atti* (1971a, containing articles by Calboli, Krenn, Niculescu, Seuren, Valesio) and *Scritti* (1972 Clivio, Giurescu, Krenn), in which a good deal of recent literature is collected or referred to.

◥4.4.2 *Componential analysis*

A very recent development of the generative approach is the componential analysis, which accounts for a much deeper level in representation. The approach is essentially semanticist, in that it interprets underlying phrase-markers in terms of meaning, and more precisely in terms of semantic features. A complete theory of description in terms of deep semantic features has been elaborated in the past few years by a group of Roman linguists, and their findings have been published in a long series of papers: Antinucci (1969), Castelfranchi - Parisi (1969), Parisi - Castelfranchi (1969), Antinucci - Crisari - Parisi (1971), D'Addio (1971), Crisari - Parisi - Puglielli (1971), Crisari (1971), Antinucci - Puglielli (1971), Castelfranchi (1971) see also the essays collected in Parisi (1975).

The whole frame of reference, which beside clusters of semantic features employs such concepts as presuppositions, performatives, predicates, much in the vein of Fillmore and Lakoff, but independently from them, has been expounded and exemplified with Italian data in Parisi - Antinucci (1973).

Recent semanticist developments of the standard transformational-generative theory are spreading at a very fast pace, and in recent times many papers have been published outside the Roman group, based chiefly on Fillmore's and Ross' insights. We can quote Conte (1972) on performatives, Renzi (1971), Cinque (1972), and some other papers contained in *Atti* (1972).

It is easily predictable that this will be the prevailing trend in the immediate future of research on Italian.

V. LEXICON

5.1 THE STRUCTURE OF THE LEXICON

There are just a few works that deal with Italian lexical devices. An important series of papers by Migliorini (1934, 1936, 1943, 1948) deals with aspects of production and examines the role of certain specific lexical morphemes, such as *-ante* (of *bracciante, lavorante*), *-trice, -a* for masculine nouns (*il profeta*). A particularly broad coverage of lexical structures is given by Hall (1948), already quoted.

Merlo (1951) and Tollemache (1954) deal with deverbatives (of the type *visita* 'visit' < *visitare* 'to visit'), and Tollemache gives a useful catalogue of relevant items. On compounds we note Tollemache (1945), Giovannelli (1967), Giurescu (1965), and Tekavčić (1967, 1970-71). Some peculiar points have received more than the usual amount of attention: such is the case of the prefix *s-*; see Devoto (1939), Brøndal (1941), Marchand (1953).

The works just quoted are most important for the data they provide on the productive devices in the Italian lexicon: almost all the processes they account for are very commonly exploited in Italian. Nevertheless we still need a more comprehensive treatment of the lexicon; a work like Guiraud's *Les structures étymologiques du lexique française* (Guiraud 1967) is still lacking, and certainly our present knowledge of historical etymology, morphology, and semantics, even if not definitive in every point, would permit at least a first attempt toward such an overall treatment (for an interesting essay in componential analysis, see Alinei 1974).

5.2 LEXICOGRAPHY

5.2.0 *Generalities*

The origins of Italian lexicography are to be traced, leaving aside some older and shorter word-lists, to the 16th century. The first vocabularies of the Italian language (the *Tre fontane* of N. Liburnio, 1526; the *Vocabulario* of F. Luna, 1536; *La fabbrica del mondo* of F. Alunno, 1546, and many similar works) clustered together throughout the 16th century, were intended chiefly to explain the vocabulary used by Dante, Petrarch, and Boccaccio (the "three fountains") and possibly by other classical authors of the "best centuries" (see Migliorini 1951: 90-105 for more details). But in fact the aim was twofold: on the one hand, rare terms and phrases, perhaps not immediately understandable to the average reader, were elucidated; on the other hand, a lexical standard pattern or model was suggested. There is no need to say that a word used by such an authority as Dante deserved full credit and could be used without any hesitation in writing prose or poetry. But the converse was also true: a word without such a prestigious pedigree could never expect to be included in a pure Italian text. This prescriptivist and puristic trend was to influence deeply all future lexicography. From then on, an Italian vocabulary was expected to be more a law book than a history book, and significantly the name of the most important foundation for lexicography, the *Accademia della Crusca*, or simply *la Crusca*, was assumed to mean the sifting out of the fine flour of the purest language from the 'bran' (the *crusca*).

5.2.1 General lexicons

The most renowned and most influential example of an Italian dictionary is the *Vocabolario degli Accademici della Crusca*, whose first edition was published in 1612 in Venice, an event which raised countless polemics, criticisms, approval and suggestions, but which also stimulated similar enterprises in Europe. Other editions followed, a second one in 1623, a third in 1691, a fourth between 1729 and 1738; the fifth and the last began in 1843 and was interrupted in 1923 (eleven volumes published, from A to O); for the criteria followed in the choice of the examples and for the main characteristics of the various editions, see Migliorini (1951: 91-101; 1960: 450-3). For the new edition of the *Crusca*, in preparation, see below, par *5.3*.

The mention of the *Vocabolario della Crusca* was by no means unnecessary: it is impossible to understand the development of Italian lexicography unless one takes into account the perpetual presence of the Crusca as a kind of bourd an always underlying reference in every speculation and work on the language, be approved or to be rejected, but never ignored or dismissed. The very word *crusca* with all its derivatives came to mean two opposite things: a warranty of good language, but also a strongly criticized purism (*cruscare, cruschevole, cruscheg giare,* and so on came all to mean 'to abandon oneself to sterile linguistic evolu tions', with a mocking overtone).

One can safely say that almost every Italian writer at least once in his life had something to say concerning the "questione della lingua" and the *Crusca*: this is the case with Leopardi, Monti, who wrote six volumes of a *Proposta di alcune correzioni ed aggiunte al vocabolario della Crusca* (Monti 1817-24), Manzoni, and so on.

Lexicographic work is especially abundant in the 19th century; here we quote only the more reputed among the many dictionaries published in this span of time: the *Vocabolario universale italiano*, published by the Tramater publishers in Naples (*Vocabolario* 1829-40), a reprint of fourth *Crusca*, but greatly improved with neologisms and technical terms; the *Vocabolario della lingua italiana* (Manuzzi 1833-40), a revision and a recasting of the *Crusca*; the two works of Gherardini (1838-40, 1852-57), the well-known Tommaseo - Bellini (1861-79) and the more reduced Fanfani (1855), Rigutini - Fanfani (1875), Petrocchi (1887-91).

Strangely enough, in spite of the living tradition indicated by the impressive list of works quoted above (a list which could easily be increased), those older monuments of erudition were never to be superseded: if we quote them, it is also because they are still today, at least some of them, useful to the language historian.

Even today, it is very common to resort to the old Tommaseo - Bellini (1861-79) when searching for the history of a word: in spite of its many faults, this large reference work remains the broadest and most comprehensive collection of words and examples.

5.2.2 *Historical lexicons*

For a satisfactory treatment of the lexicon of a language at least two kinds of dictionaries are needed: a historical one, featuring a comprehensive list of words observed in every phase of the history of the language, a full chronology of the usage of every word including of course the date of the first known occurrence, and possibly an etymology of the word; and a descriptive one, which accounts for the current usage of the language, featuring technical and special meanings, phonological patterns of every entry, indications on different levels and usage registers, and so on. Obviously, the aims of the two types are complementary: a foreign student concerned with present-day language would have but little interest in using a historical dictionary. Unfortunately, this empirical distinction was never properly drawn in Italian lexicography, and every author of a dictionary strives to straddle the fence. Almost every dictionary published so far displays a bit of modern usage and a bit of classical citation: that means that the old-fashioned type of view on dictionary making is preserved, improved of course by a more or less generous addition of modern forms, technical terms, neologisms, foreign words. As a consequence of this original lexicographic sin, committed again and again, today we are still lacking a complete and reliable historical dictionary (as, for instance, the Oxford *New English dictionary on historical principles*), as well as a *dictionnaire de l'usage courant* (as the French ones, or as the ones many unwritten languages have: a Menomini or an Igbo dictionary would be automatically a dictionary of current usage; sometimes the weight of tradition is more properly a burden!).

Undoubtedly, the largest and most comprehensive modern dictionary of Italian is Battaglia (1961-), which is both a historical record and one of modern usage. Examples are drawn from the whole span of Italian literature, with unusual coverage and meticulous care in the choice of sources, all quoted according to the most reliable editions and with full references; the samples of texts for every entry are quite extensive, and brief etymological information is appended. The work is still in progress (eight volumes so far, comprising approximately half of the whole work); after the untimely death of Professor Battaglia, the work is being carried on by a team of co-workers, directed by G. Bàrberi-Squarotti. In spite of some strange omissions in the entries as well as in the sampling of texts, the Battaglia is a very useful tool. although it needs still to be implemented with the Tommaseo-Bellini (1861-79).

Of a wide-scoped *Vocabolario della lingua italiana* edited by the Accademia d'Italia, only the first volume (*A-C*) was published (*Vocabolario* 1941). With the defeat of Fascism, the Accademia d'Italia was dissolved, and obviously the work stopped. In view of the scanty value of the published part, there is no reason to regret this fact.

A monumental encyclopedic work with deep implications for the history of the language is the *Enciclopedia Dantesca* (*Enciclopedia* 1970-); along with a full treatment of every topic related to Dante and his works, the *Enciclopedia* includes a very detailed "*Lessico dantesco*"; it is worth saying that the lexicon goes far beyond a mere list of forms, and pays unusual attention to syntactic developments and constructions, as well as to semantic values.

5.2.3 Contemporary usage

5.2.3.0 Generalities

As we have seen, the attitude towards contemporary usage has very rarely been unbiased; the view that contemporary usage is intrinsically neither good nor bad but simply a fact to be described as such, seems to be quite recent.

Obviously, common sense is not an achievement of modern linguistics, and there have always been illuminated writers and grammarians — even if the latter were fewer than the former — to defend the rights of current usage. But this

defense has usually been rather rare, and in general the very word *neologism*
has been used as a brand of shame, ignoring the rather trivial fact that languages
are unceasingly creating new words, rejecting older ones and incorporating foreign
words (when useful). As a matter of fact, the main activity of grammarians and
linguists in the last century was to prepare long lists and dictionaries of neologisms
to be avoided in writing and speaking (see Zolli 1971-72 for useful materials and
references; for a specimen of this literature, see Fanfani - Arlìa 1877). This attitude has not yet completely disappeared (see Fochi 1964, 1966; Pestelli 1967;
Pestelli is a rare specimen of a purist endowed with a delicate sense of humor.
and his essays are worth reading, even if the position he defends is rather
extreme). But the prevailing attitude is exemplified in the works of B. Migliorini. He labels it *neopurism*. It is an illuminated purism which does not refuse
neologisms as such, but tries to recast them according to the shape of the
language, and tries to avoid unnecessary proliferation of foreign words (if an
Italian word is at hand, why borrow its counterpart in a foreign language?).
This attitude is widely expounded in many of Migliorini's essays (Migliorini
1938, 1941, 1957, 1962) and in many articles published in *Lingua nostra*.

5.2.3.1 *Dictionaries of contemporary usage*

The broadest dictionary declaredly based on contemporary usage is the *Dizionario enciclopedico italiano* (*Enciclopedia* 1955-61), which properly speaking
is an encyclopedia, with a highly developed and highly reliable lexicographic
section. Attention is also paid to phonetic and etymological aspects. Especially
because of the large selection of technical terminology, the *Enciclopedia* (1955-
1961) is one of the best reference works available at present. Contributors
include some of the best-known contemporary linguists and lexicographers.
    Many one-volume general dictionaries are allegedly based on current usage.
From a continuous revision of Cappuccini (1916), Cappuccini - Migliorini (1945)
and then Migliorini (1965) were derived, keeping closer and closer to current
usage. Much on the same lines, an appendix on neologisms added by Migliorini
to the eigth edition (1942) of Panzini (1905) has been growing, edition after
edition, until it formed a separate volume (Migliorini 1963).
    The collection was intended to draw selectively from the large mass of
neologisms and foreign words which entered contemporary Italian through
the mass-media chiefly since World War 2. To remain useful, this kind of work
ought to be revised almost every year: as it is, Migliorini (1963), is largely outdated and many of the "parole nuove" are now obsolete, or have since under-
gone deep changes in form and meaning. A highly reliable reference book
is Devoto - Oli (1967): in its somewhat abridged second edition (Devoto - Oli
1971) it includes some 75.000 entries, drawn from many specialized subfields,

chiefly scientific ones. Passerini Tosi (1969) devotes a lot of space to current usage, and can be considered the more complete of the two from this point of view.

A set of important features is displayed by the recent Zingarelli (1970), the tenth edition of a popular but very conventional work. The new edition has been completely recast, with an innovative effort quite unusual in the field of modern dictionaries. Literary sources have been examined anew; to each entry a phonemic transcription (designed by P. Fiorelli) has been appended, as well as a brief but very reliable etymological note (by M. Cortelazzo, with the help of P. Zamboni and P. Zolli); the choice of entries is very wide in scope, and many technical and foreign terms have been included, for a total of 118,000 entries. For the first time a small-size dictionary has been produced as a joint work of a team of experts in different technical fields. As we know, all previous dictionaries were compiled almost singlehandedly through the lifelong efforts of a single or possibly a couple of scholars. In spite of minor shortcomings, the new Zingarelli is the best current dictionary, and it is to be hoped that new improved editions will follow along the same lines.

5.2.3.2 *Special languages*

Most dictionaries of specialized terminology (arts, crafts, and so on) in view of their merely practical aims are devoid of linguistic momentum. An exception worth noting is the *Dizionario di marina* (*Dizionario* 1937) to which as skilled an etymologist as A. Prati contributed. A survey of special dictionaries is to be found in Migliorini (1951: 117-22). The series "Glossari di lingua contemporanea", directed by C. Bascetta, is intended to supplement current dictionaries in selected subfields: so far ten volumes have been published: Bascetta (1964), Medici (1965), Sabbatucci (1965), Gonnelli (1966), Plebe (1966), Caramella (1967), Carlà (1967), Medici (1967), Mistrorigo (1968), Cardona (1969a). Every volume is very simple in character, and accounts briefly for some 200-400 special words in its field. E. Ferrero (1972) surveys some 2500 slang and jargon forms from a very specific field, the speech of the underworld. The book is intended for a large audience, but it deserves full credit for the wide choice of items from all possible sources and for its largely accurate presentation.

Also useful, in view of the scarcity of published material, but much less sophisticated than the former, is Cantagalli (1972), a dictionary of ambiguous words (with a second, obscene meaning).

An interesting juridical dictionary has been announced, the *Vocabolario giuridico italiano*, directed by P. Fiorelli. In view of the twofold skills of its editor, as a jurist and as a linguist, the project is promising (see Fiorelli 1947 for the preliminary plan).

5.2.4 *Etymological studies*

5.2.4.1 *Etymological dictionaries*

Apart from etymological evidence on Italian available from Meyer-Lübke's *Romanisches etymologisches Wörterbuch*, for a long time the only etymological dictionary was Zambaldi (1889); other attempts were completely devoid of scientific value and were rather amateurish (a case in point is Pianigiani 1936-37). In recent times no less than five etymological dictionaries of Italian were published, all of them in Italian, in a span of a few years: Battisti-Alessio (1950-57), Migliorini - Duro (1950), Prati (1951), Olivieri (1953), Devoto (1966); their size ranges from the five bulging volumes of Battisti-Alessio to the slim Migliorini - Duro of 600 pages (for an evaluation of the first four of them cf. Vuolo 1954).

Obviously, the lack of a reliable and well-grounded historical lexicography has considerably hindered etymological research: it is very difficult to give a well-balanced etymological assessment of a word whose external history (i.e., not the purely phonetic development) remains unknown, unless one is satisfied with a mere statement of the remote ancestor of the word. A case in point would be the countless modern scientific terms of artificial Graeco-Latin origin, like *telephone, telegram*, and so on, whose remote origin is utterly irrelevant.

Only Battisti-Alessio and Prati give chronological data, but sometimes in a very desultory and unreliable fashion. As for the choice of sources, it is regrettable that, much in the vein of the lexicographic tradition, literary works are by far more exploited than scientific works, and many authors of science, crafts, and travels were never exhaustively surveyed from this point of view. That means that entire fields of specialized, technical, scientific or simply foreign lexicon are almost unknown to us, in view of the more conservative character of literature as against science. An extensive survey of the extremely flourishing "travelology" of the 14th-16th centuries, for instance, cluding translations and documents, would afford a great deal of knowledge n the relations among Italian, on the one hand, and foreign languages (Portuguese, Spanish, Middle and Far Eastern languages) on the other, throughout such a brilliant period as the Age of Discoveries. On the contrary, beyond the common core of Romance origin, the Italian lexicon is still inadequately known, chiefly when less familiar languages are involved.

The two larger dictionaries, Battisti - Alessio and Prati, do not overlap, but each one requires the other; Prati surveys about 18.000 items, is more reliable as far as sources are concerned, and is more personal in judgment; it gives broad coverage to dialects, slang, jargon, onomatopoeia, and in general to words with a more complicated history, according to the author's personal interests and skills. As a minor point, Prati is also the only dictionary which gives biblio-graphical references: with others, it is impossible to ascertain at first glance if an etymology is commonly accepted by the majority of scholars, or if it is a personal achievement or hypothesis. Battisti - Alessio includes no less than 82.000 entries, with many dialect forms and a high number of modern tech-nical terms. One of the coauthors, G. Alessio, has provided in later years a large series of addenda and observations to *DEI* (as this dictionary is current-ly referred to), see Alessio (1957-58, 1962).

Olivieri (1953) and Migliorini - Duro (1950) are rather simplified and are intended to be a first approach to Italian etymology; Migliorini - Duro (1950) is more reliable and gives only etyma traceable with certainty; Olivieri includes many data on toponomastics. Devoto (1966) attempts to trace every entry to its Proto-Indo-European form; for instance, the etymology of the Italian word *luna* 'moon' is not limited to the obvious statement "from Lat. *luna*", but tries to give a further characterization of this *luna* in PIE terms: let us quote the entry in its entirety:

luna, lat. *luna*, da **louksna*, tipo diffuso di derivato con signif. vicino al nome d'agente, dalla rad. LEUK (v. Luce, Lume). Dal punto di vista della forma la parola compare nel-le aree iranica, tocarica, baltica, e, anche, in quella slava, baltica e armena; dal punto di vista del signif. la definiz. come "la lucente" appare anche nel gr. *seléné* e nel sanscrito *candrama-* che sono di altra origine. (Devoto 1966 *s.v.*).

In this way one would have a sort of longitudinal cross-section of the Italian lexicon which goes back to and sometimes beyond the oldest witnessed phases of Indo-European languages.

Unfortunately, this method does not improve our knowledge of the Italian lexicon; around the Indo-European core, or more precisely beside the core of immediate and obvious Indo-European origin, with the exception of obviously foreign words, there still remains a thick layer of words of dubious origin, and it is too bad that in these cases Devoto resorts to a kind of off-the-cuff explan-ation, calling for blending, analogy, onomatopoeia, and so on. For example, he explains *freccia* 'arrow' as a blending of Fr. *flèche* and It. *fretta* 'haste', and *baldracca* 'whore' as a blending of *Baldacco* 'Baghdad' and *baracca* 'barrack'

It remains that at least a compact — to say nothing of a large-sized — reliable etymological dictionary which satisfies modern scientific criteria, is still lacking, and surely this could not be the work of a single scholar (see now Zolli 1975).

Among its features, this future dictionary should include:

(a) a more careful choice of samples; the higher frequency lexicon, as it appears, for instance, from Bortolini - Tagliavini - Zampolli (1972), ought to be included in its entirety, as a basic core: too often etymological dictionaries inform lavishly on rare and peregrine words, and say almost nothing about more common ones;

(b) the dating of the first attestation of a word, determined as precisely as possible, according to our present knowledge (a date "16th century" is too vague);

(c) the proper etymology must distinguish among different degrees of certainty, from obvious to hypothetical: it is quite misleading to present an obvious statement and a farfetched hypothesis side-by-side on the same level;

(d) short bibliographical references;

(e) a full or at least satisfactory treatment of the meaning of the items concerned; too often only the history of the *signifiant* is sketched in the so-called phonetic etymologies;

(f) an adequate treatment of lesser-known languages: any language outside a restricted circle is ill-treated in etymological dictionaries; a case in point is the Oriental section in W. von Wartburg's *Französisches etymologisches Wörterbuch* (see Bausani - Cardona 1970).

5.2.4.2 *Special studies*

It would be very difficult and probably pointless to survey in too much detail the impressive list of etymological contributions to Italian. A good number of them is quoted, under appropriate headings, in Hall (1958); another useful reference device is the yearly index of *Lingua nostra*, which lists all the words discussed in this journal (up to 1959 a separate index volume also exists; see Crocetti 1961).

Many Italian scholars have dedicated a large portion of their academic endeavor to the elucidation of the lexicon from a historical point of view: B. Migliorini (see Migliorini 1957, for a bibliography and a selection of articles), A. Pagliaro (whose contributions to Italian are scattered through a large eclectic production; the references are given by Cardona 1969b), C. Tagliavini (a collection of essays with bibliography is forthcoming; see Tagliavini 1976), and among younger scholars, M. Cortelazzo, G. Folena, G.B. Pellegrini, E. Peruzzi.

The history of Italian etymology partially overlaps with the history of Romance etymology. A broader treatment of the work in this field, to which many excellent scholars outside of Italy have been contributing (B.E. Vidos, H. & R. Kahane, and many others) is to be expected from such a prestigious investigator of Romance etymology as Yakov Malkiel.

In another special field, loanwords, we can mention the impressive series of papers on Arabic elements by G.B. Pellegrini, reprinted recently in Pellegrini

(1972; see Cardona 1973b), and two monographs on French (Hope 1971) and English (Klajn 1972). Beccaria (1968) and Cardona (1973a) focus on Spanish and Portuguese elements, respectively, in the 16th-17th centuries; but, since the core of these loanwords has survived to this day, the two can also be used in the study of the contemporary lexicon.

The Italian standard language is less inclined to receive loanwords then the dialects: it was possible for M. Cortelazzo to write a broad monograph on Modern Greek loanwords in Venetian (Cortelazzo 1970); but a similar monograph would hardly be possible for Standard Italian, in which Modern Greek elements are almost non-existent. Arabic and Turkish elements are by far more abundant in the dialects, especially Southern ones (by the way, there is still no monograph on Turkish loanwords in Italian). This is easily explainable in view of the more conservative character of the standard language as opposed to the dialects (from which follows a trend toward a "purer", more classical use, untinged by colloquial forms and phrases), and also in view of the peripheral character of contacts with foreigners, and even with conquerors in Italy: travel, exchanges, and even dominations remained restricted to a single ethnic group or region and did not effect the whole country (Spaniards in Naples, Muslims in Sicily, commercial exchanges between Venice and the Middle East, and so on); contrast with this the pervasive character of Turkish elements in Roumanian or Modern Greek.

A specific cross-section of the Italian lexicon, the words pertaining to religion, to the calendar, to liturgy, and so on, has been lavishly treated and traced to its origins by Tagliavini (1963). The etymology of proper nouns has been treated extensively in a handy reference work by Tagliavini (1955-57); semantic developments from proper to common nouns (of the type Lat. *Cicero* > It. *Cicerone* > It. *cicerone* 'guide') are fully accounted for in a now classical work by Migliorini (1927), recently reprinted (1968) in an expanded edition (see Prosdocimi 1971 for a review).

Especially in the past few years much emphasis has been placed on new trends in special vocabularies (broadcasting, television, sports) and many contributions have been published on single points: see for instance Pettenati (1953, 1955) for medical and pharmaceutical terminology, Medici (1961) for television, Bascetta (1962) (a rather comprehensive monograph), for sports, Medici (1966) for football, Menarini (1956) for cinema. A topic which appeals particularly to linguists is the language of advertising; although they are not devoted exclusively to the lexicon, we shall quote Folena (1964), Altieri Biagi (1965), Castagnotto (1970; more theoretically oriented), and a long series of papers by M. Medici, collected in Medici (1973); this work includes a complete bibliography on this topic. For the special field of euphemism see Galli de' Paratesi (1964). Widɫak (1970, 1972), and Cantagalli (1972) quoted above. See also paragraph 8.3.

5.3 COMPUTERIZED ANALYSIS

The increasing bulk of lexicographic undertakings in recent years makes it
worthwhile to dedicate a separate section to computerized analysis.

Of course, we agree with the remarks by M. Alinei (1969: 74), who stresses
the fact that from a theoretical point of view, computerized lexicography involves methods no different from traditional lexicography, and accordingly
the mere use of a computer could not be considered a new *Deus ex machina
(electronica)*. But is also true that the entire range of analysis dealing with,
for instance, mathematical properties of a certain corpus of data, would hardly be feasible without the aid of electronic devices. The fact that a purely
technical device makes feasible what would be otherwise only imaginable vests
— so to speak — the whole of the computerized methods with a sort of theoretical rehabilitation.

The first application of computers to Italian lexicography is represented by
the inverse dictionary of M. Alinei (1962), which takes the entries of Migliorini -
Duro (1950) as its starting point. The only shortcoming of this pioneer work
is the reduced number of entries over against the adopted source. That means
that findings and percentages cannot be assumed to represent more than a
portion of the contemporary Italian lexicon. But of course the author intended
his inverse dictionary more as a first methodological step than as a definitive
reference work. In 1965, as the first application to a literary text, a concordance
of Dante's *Commedia* was published (Alighieri 1965); this extremely useful
work, sponsored by the Italian branch of IBM, had very limited diffusion, in
view of its non-commercial nature.

Since 1965, several projects in the computerized analysis of Italian have been
begun (see Duro 1967b, 1966b, 1971; Tagliavini 1968, Duro - Zampolli 1968).

Most important in size and scope are the two undertakings of the Italian
Accademia della Crusca (which resumed its activity in 1964): a *Historical
dictionary of the Italian language* and a *Thesaurus of the early beginnings
(till 1375)*. The relevant feature of the two long-awaited (and perhaps long-
to-be-awaited) works is the extensive use of computers. Filing cards, drawn
from a corpus of over 100 million samples, will be arranged with the aid of
a computer; this routine entails a bulk of work that would be utterly unfeas-
ible manually, and it eliminates a great percentage of possible errors. The publication of the first of the two, the *Thesaurus*, which will fill a very serious gap
in presently available lexicographic sources, is announced for 1975 (the activity
in progress of the Accademia has been surveyed annually by Duro 1966a,
1967a, 1968, 1969, 1970, where lists of key-punched texts are also given).
As a preliminary work to the *Thesaurus*, a collection of lexical listings (*Spogli elettronici dell'italiano delle Origini e del Duecento*), directed by M. A.

Alinei (1968-) is being published. So far 13 volumes have been published (including works by D. Alighieri, B. Latini, B. Giamboni, Jacopone da Todi, etc.); a total of fifty volumes covering about 5 million words is scheduled; other series that focus on syntactic and morphologic features, are also planned, in this connection. Recently, a second series of the *Spogli* has been started, which is devoted exclusively to modern written Italian (Moravia, Cassola, Calvino, etc.).

In 1967, the Accademia della Crusca began publishing samples of concordances of single authors, chiefly in the format of offset reproductions from computer listings (see *Accademia della Crusca* 1967, 1968, 1969, 1971).

So far for the computerized analysis of diachronic Italian. The most interesting work in contemporary Italian is the statistical dictionary Bortolini - Tagliavini - Zampolli (1972). It is based on a large corpus of modern written prose (plays, newspapers, textbooks, and so on), collected anew for the purpose (on the basic criteria underlying the choice of texts and the methods, see Bortolini - Zampolli 1971). The first 5000 words of contemporary Italian are listed according to their rank and frequency. This dictionary is an extremely welcome work: for the first time it allows for an unbiased insight into the very core of the Italian lexicon, as it is mirrored in real written usage. This statistical evidence can be used in a broad range of applications: in preparing basic language courses, in stylistic analyses, etc.

Another frequency dictionary of Italian words has been announced, by A. Juilland, scheduled as the fifth in a series of Romance frequency dictionaries (the French, Spanish, and Roumanian ones have already been published); judging from the bulk of the published volumes (ca. 500 pages) it seems the Italian volume will not supersede the Bortolini - Tagliavini - Zampolli (1972).

VI. LANGUAGE ACQUISITION

The first scientific contribution to the study of first-language acquisition is to be credited to G. Frontali (Frontali 1943-44); although his observations on speech-sound acquisition are rather desultory and somewhat inadequate, he gives some useful insights into the psychological side of language development (for a more recent survey by the same author, see Frontali 1962).

As was customary in former literature on language acquisition, evidence was drawn from diaristic records of the speech development of the author's child. From the same kind of source stems a more detailed monograph by W. von Raffler Engel (1964). The author focuses on the "melodic" aspects of pre-language, suggesting that children are able to produce and respond to a melodic utterance sooner than to a verbal utterance. The development of the first core of the phonological system in children is also studied, and, although evidence seems still too scarce for further generalizations, the author is inclined to find support for the Jakobsonian hypothesis of development. Data on mere articulatory aspects are presented by Battacchi *et alii* (1964, 1968-69).

A specific case for the coexistence of phonemic systems in bilingual children (Italian and Danish) is treated by Francescato (1961; see Francescato 1954). Other occasional remarks on Italian examples are scattered through further works by Francescato (see Francescato 1970 for references). An interesting case of trilingualism is reported by Francescato (1971).

From a systematic longitudinal survey of the speech of a group of children stems a long series of papers published by a research team sponsored by the Italian National Research Council; see Parisi - Antinucci (1970), Antinucci - Parisi (1971), Parisi - Antinucci (1973, 1975, 1976), Volterra (1972).

The most relevant feature shared by these papers is the systematic presentation of first-hand evidence, carefully collected and checked throughout a span of time, and cast in an explanatory framework which makes strong assumptions on the kind of mental processes involved; the approach chosen by Antinucci, Parisi, Volterra and other co-workers is a semanticist one, according to the comprehensive descriptive model expounded in Parisi - Antinucci (1973).

VII. APPLIED LINGUISTICS

In surveying existing literature on applied linguistics in connection with Italian, one must remember that any applied method involves a great deal of scientific knowledge of the language concerned. For instance, the lack of a dictionary of basic Italian was a serious handicap which hindered the preparation of handbooks. From a simple experiment carried out by Jeremić (1969) we can see that the aim of giving a compact stock of high-frequency words has never been achieved. The four major handbooks of Italian published in Yugoslavia contain 8000 words altogether but only 275 of them overlap in all four.

Recently it has been possible to overcome these shortcomings, with the publication of Bortolini-Tagliavini-Zampolli (1972) which lists the first 5000 words of basic Italian.

We have already quoted studies on contrastive phonology (cf. par 3.6).

Only one comprehensive contrastive grammar exists: Agard - Di Pietro (1965b), on Italian and English.

Portions of grammar are dealt with by De Boer (1926), Marchand (1955), Carlsson (1966), Valesio (1967c), Stobitzer (1968), Carlsson (1969), Saronne (1971), Clivio (1972), Niculescu (1971).

A large number of Italian examples are quoted in two rather different works, Wandruszka (1969), which focuses on problems of translation from literary texts (English, German, French, Spanish, Portuguese, and Italian) and Di Pietro (1971a), a theoretical handbook for contrastive analysis.

Two practical treatments of Italian grammar consistent with linguistic tenets are Hall (1961) and Hall (1964a).

There are two journals focused entirely or partially on problems in applied linguistics, and Italian; both of them are published in Italy. The *Rassegna italiana di linguistica applicata* (Rome 1969-), directed by R. Titone, and formerly entitled *Homo loquens* (Padua 1967-1968), deals chiefly with the teaching of Italian as first and second language.

More theoretically oriented is the new-born *Studi di linguistica teorica e applicata* (Bologna 1972 -) directed by L. Heilmann and E. Arcaini. The 1970 conference of the Società Italiana di Linguistica was also devoted to the teaching of Italian; in *Atti* (1971b) data on the teaching of Italian abroad are collected. A detailed survey of recent work in applied linguistics, especially in connection with Italian, is offered by Berruto - Calleri - Sobrero (1972).

VIII. SOCIOLINGUISTICS

8.0 GENERALITIES

Owing to the prevailing attention paid to standard forms of Italian, sociolinguistics studies, which involve consideration of different levels of usage
and of different social contexts, are obviously not yet fully developed in
Italy, nor, at least to my knowledge, abroad, as far as Italian is concerned.
The whole situation is highly complicated by the peculiar relationships between standard language and dialects, and it is difficult to separate sociolinguistic aspects of the one from the other.

Presently, the best work is being carried on in dialect-speaking areas. In
recent times sociolinguistically oriented theses have been accepted only in
those Italian departments where there is a strong tradition in dialectological
studies, chiefly in Turin and Padua; in Italy sociolinguistics as such is not
to be found among courses offered by linguistics departments, and the next
best approximations are to be found in the more illuminated dialectology.

8.1 RELATIONSHIPS BETWEEN THE STANDARD LANGUAGE AND THE DIALECTS

Leaving a more detailed treatment of this topic to a separate volume on Italian
dialects, I mention only the two articles by Pellegrini (1960, 1962; the first
included with other essays in Pellegrini 1973), and the very accurate methodological reflections by Berruto (1971). Much evidence, as well as many critical
observations are brought up by Grassi (1964, 1965b; in answer to De Mauro
1963). Surveys of bilingual and trilingual situations are given by Braga (1969)
and Denison (1969). Some reports on sociolinguistic problems involved in the
teaching of Standard Italian to dialectophones are to be found in *Atti* (1971b).

We have already (*2.2*) quoted De Mauro (1963); in its treatment it displays
a certain trend toward a sociolinguistic approach, in that sociolinguistic factors
are also taken into account; but apart from the shortcomings we have already

pointed out, many assumptions are also questionable from a sociolinguistic point of view (see a well-documented reply in the two papers by Grassi, quoted above), for instance in the use of statistical evidence.

8.2 THE SO-CALLED ITALIANO POPOLARE

One of the first attempts to study a non-literary variety of Italian was undertaken by L. Spitzer. He set out to elaborate the concept of an Italian *Umgangssprache* in which — and this was his fatal flaw — the Italian national character would be best mirrored. Spitzer drew his data from a large collection of letters written by semi-literate Italians, on the assumption that those texts could represent a kind of unsophisticated and untampered transcription of the real colloquial language of non-cultivated people (Spitzer 1921, 1922).

The same concept of *Umgangssprache* was adopted by Rüegg (1956; see the reviews by Folena 1958a and Grassi 1958), who strove to define a variety of non-standard Italian that was distinct from the dialects, and was used in everyday interactions. Rüegg gave useful lists of lexical items, pertaining to colloquial usage in every region of Italy.

In more recent times, it has became almost commonplace to speak of an "Italiano popolare", an *Umgangssprache* which is assumed to have precise lexical as well as morphological and syntactical connotations all over Italy.

One of the merits of De Mauro (1963) was indeed to have raised the question of an "Italiano popolare unitario" as opposed to the standard language. But unfortunately he did not give any adequate characterization of this new linguistic entity; the scattered data he gives in his text refer sometimes to regional Italian, sometimes to the dialects. That means that he gives no definite set of features that characterizes a precise variety of language unambiguously. As it stands, the label *Italiano popolare* seems more a stimulating hypothesis than a factual reality. In subsequent works, De Mauro has often called for a description for this "Italiano popolare", without any further attempt to define his framework more precisely. The only information we can glean from De Mauro (1970) is that the "Italiano popolare" is mirrored in a corpus of written record (mostly autobiographical materials, written by semiliterates or collected by others; for one of those texts, Montaldi's *Autobiografie della leggera* (Montaldi 1961), see Valesio 1961). But the author does not apply all the necessary methodological care required for the handling of an essentially spoken language studied only in its written form. How would we be able to decide whether a certain written feature is to be assigned to the idiolect of the writer, or is due to an imperfect knowledge of the standard written norm?

A stronger attempt toward the definition of an adequate concept of "Italiano popolare" has been recently made by Cortelazzo (1972), who defines it as "il tipo di italiano imperfettamente acquisito da chi ha per madrelingua il dialetto" (the kind of Italian imperfectly acquired by native dialect speakers; Cortelazzo 1972: 11). After having established a corpus of the few written monuments of "Italiano popolare", Cortelazzo gives a preliminary list of its features with full discussion. Up to now, Cortelazzo's attempt is the best treatment of the topic. But more relevant results could be reached leaving aside written transcriptions and planning a completely different routine, collecting spoken data, and transcribing actual utterances.

8.3 THE INFLUENCE OF MASS-MEDIA

Among the scattered and scanty contributions on the influence of the mass-media on standard language, one of the first studies made led to the slim monograph by O. Fracastoro Martini (1951) on the influence of radio broadcasting on common usage. This was the first attention paid to such a broad and far-reaching phenomenon. Unfortunately, no deeper treatment of the topic has since followed. The influence of television from 1954 to 1966 has been studied by De Mauro (1968; television language *in se* had already been studied by Medici 1961), but the author's findings concerning an allegedly deep-rooted influence of technical language seem to be supported by no concrete evidence. As Sobrero (1971) has shown, the whole influence limits itself to a handful of technical terms.

The sociolinguistic feedback of advertising has been surveyed in many articles, chiefly by Medici since 1952 (Medici 1952, 1973); the most recent sociolinguistic survey is Sobrero (1973).

Sociolinguistic aspects of newspaper language have been dealt with by Amerio Pompei (1969) and recently by Dardano (1973), in a comprehensive monograph; aspects of political information are offered by Di Maria (1969).

Here again, we still need a comprehensive monograph on the overall influence of the mass-media on contemporary Italian, and it is high time that the different insights and findings elaborated so far be combined in a synthetic overview (detailed bibliographical information on the topics treated in this section is now readily available: see Còveri 1973, Marcato Politi 1974 on Italian sociolinguistics in general; Beccaria 1973, Medici 1975 on mass-media).

IX. STYLISTICS

It is only for the sake of (relative) completeness that we try to list a few items on stylistics here. It is extremely difficult to define a section of stylistic studies on Italian, in view of the scarcity of rigorous definitions of the field.

Gossen (1954) studies the devices available in Italian for what he calls "reinforcement" (*Hervorhebung*): reduplication, syntactic emphasis, and so on; Gossen (1956) and Rüsch (1963) deal with direct address and exclamations. Gossen (1963) handles the use of questions as a stylistic device.

Two different aspects of metaphor have been studied by Junker (1957; the origin and spreading of metaphors from different domains of the external world) and by Pasini (1968; on metaphor as a linguistic concept).

The perhaps only comprehensive study on phonosymbolics and phonostylistics in Italian, the handbook by Valesio on alliteration (Valesio 1967a), deserves special mention.

A comprehensive handbook of stylistic devices has been published recently by L. Galdi (1972). The catalogue is accurate, but the depth of analysis is still inadequate, and the treatment is not very satisfactory.

The application of stylistic analysis to literary texts has been more successful, in view of the more rewarding character of literary analyses. The treatment of literary texts seems to exceed somewhat the scope of a strictly linguistic survey. But we shall quote at least the analyses on single authors carried out by Rosiello (1963, 1965; on Montale) and by Stussi (1961; on Pascoli), and the collection of essays edited by Bandini et alii (1966), in view of the linguistic relevance of the method adopted. Baldelli (1965) is an experiment in the study of stylistic variants in literary texts, carried out in the vein of a historian of the language: the author shows how the choice of certain variants in recent editions of novels and short stories by such modern authors as Cassola, Testori, etc. mirrors a deliberate trend toward a more "standard" type of Italian.

Many contributions to stylistics problems are to be found in two Italian journals, *Lingua e stile* and *Strumenti critici* (Turin).

X. BIBLIOGRAPHY

Accademia della Crusca (ed.)
1967   *Concordanze degli Inni sacri di A. Manzoni; testo, lista di frequenza, lista di concordanza* (Firenze: Accademia della Crusca). [offset reproduction ot computer listings]
1968   *Novella del grasso legnaiuolo nella redazione del codice Palatino 200; testo, frequenze, concordanze* (Firenze: Accademia della Crusca).
1969   *Saggio delle concordanze del Canzoniere di Francesco Petrarca (La Canzone "Italia mia"; rimario del Canzoniere)* (Firenze: Accademia della Crusca).
1971   *Concordanze del Canzoniere di Francesco Petrarca; concordanze, frequenze, rimario,* 2 vols. (Firenze: Accademia della Crusca).
1972   *Indice dei testi sottoposti a spoglio lessicale fino al 30 settembre 1972* (Firenze: Accademia della Crusca). [dittoed]

Aebischer, P.
1960   "La finale -e du féminin pluriel italien, étude de stratigraphie linguistique", *SLI* 1: 5-48.
1961   "La finale -i des pluriels italiens et ses origines", *SLI* 2: 73-111.

Agard, F. B. - R. J. Di Pietro
1965a   *The sounds of English and Italian* (Chicago - London: University of Chicago Press).
1965b   *The grammatical structures of English and Italian* (Chicago - London: University of Chicago Press).

Alarcos Llorach, E.
⁰1951   *Gramática estructural según la escuela de Copenhague y con especial atención a la lengua española* (Madrid: Gredos).

Alessio, G.
1957-58   *Postille al "Dizionario etimologico italiano"* (= *Quaderni linguistici dell'Istituto di Glottologia dell'Università di Napoli* 3-4) (Roma: Officine grafiche meridionali). [cf. Battisti - Alessio (1950-57)]
1962   "Nuove postille al *Dizionario etimologico italiano*", *BCSS* 6 (= *Saggi e ricerche in memoria di E. Li Gotti* 1): 59-110. [cf. Battisti - Alessio (1950-57)]

Alighieri, D.
1965   *La divina commedia; testo, concordanze, lessici, rimario, indici* (Pisa: IBM Italia). [no author's name is given; mentioned are the names of C. Tagliavini, U. Bortolini, G. Anguillara, G. Caldara, P.L. Ridolfi, G. Tagliavini] [not for sale]

Alinei, M.
1962   *Dizionario inverso italiano con indici e liste di frequenza delle terminazioni* (The Hague - Paris: Mouton).

48

1966   "Appunti per un'analisi strutturale di alcuni tipi sintattici italiani", *LeSt* 1: 281-303.

1968   *Spogli elettronici dell'italiano delle Origini e del Duecento* (The Hague - Paris: Mouton) [From 1971: (Bologna: Il Mulino).]

1969   "Lessico e grammatica generativa", in *Atti* ⹁1969a: 73-96).

1970a   "Primi appunti per una descrizione generativo-ᵗransformazionale del nesso temporale", in *Atti* (1970: 13-22).

1970b   "Il tipo sintagmatico 'quel matto di Giorgio' ", in *Atti* (1970: 1-12).

1974   *La struttura del lessico* (Bologna: Il Mulino).

Alisova, T. [B.]

1965   "Relative limitative e relative esplicative nell'italiano popolare", *SFI* 23: 299-333.

1967   "Studi di sintassi italiana", *SFI* 25: 223-313.

1971   *Očerki sintaksisa sovremennogo ital'janskogo jazyka (semantičeskaja i grammatičeskaja struktura prostogo predloženija)* (Moskva: Izdatel'stvo Moskovskogo universiteta).

1972   *Strutture semantiche e sintattiche della proposizione semplice in italiano* (Firenze: Sansoni). [An improved version of Alisova (1971).]

Alisova, T. B. - Cerdanceva

1962   *Ital'janskij jazyk; grammatičeskij očerk, literaturnye teksty s kommentarijami i slovarem* [The Italian language; a grammatical outline and literary texts together with notes and vocabulary] (Moskva: Izdatel'stvo Moskovskogo universiteta).

Altieri Biagi, M. L.

1965   "Note sulla lingua della pubblicità", *LN* 26: 86-93.

Alunno, F.

1546   *La fabbrica del mondo di M.F.A. da Ferrara, nella quale si contengono tutte le voci di Dante, del Petrarca, del Boccaccio, et d'altri buoni autori,* ... con le quali si possono scrivendo isprimere i concetti dell'huomo di qualunque cosa creata (Venetia: N. de Boscarini).

Ambrosini, R.

1960   "L'uso dei tempi storici nell'italiano antico", *ID* 24: 13-124. [republished in: R. Ambrosini, *Strutture e parole* (Palermo: Flaccovio 1970), pp. 113-202]

Ambroso, S.

1969   "I nomi composti in italiano: basi sintattiche (schema)", in *Atti* (1969a: 97-98).

Amerio, P. - T. Pompei

1969   "Contributi sperimentali all'analisi del lessico giornalistico politico italiano dal punto di vista psicosociolinguistico", in *Giornate* (1969: 315-334). [English translation, pp. 335-351]

Antinucci, F.

1969b   "Aspetti della quantificazione in italiano", in *Atti* (1969b: 171-191).

1970   "Note del curatore", in: Noam Chomsky, *Le strutture della sintassi*, traduzione, introduzione e note di F. Antinucci (Bari: Laterza), pp. 177-201.

Antinucci, F. - M. Crisari - D. Parisi

1971   "Analisi semantica di alcuni verbi italiani", *SLI* 3: 23-46.

Antinucci, F. - D. Parisi

1971   "Primi risultati di uno studio sullo sviluppo linguistico infantile", in *Atti* (1971a: 469-489).

1973   "Early language acquisition: a model and some data", in *Studies of child language development* (Ed: Ch. A. Ferguson - D. I. Slobin) (New York: Holt, Rinehart & Winston).

49

Antinucci, F. - A. Puglielli
1971   "Struttura della quantificazione", in *Atti* (1971a: 47-62).
Arce, J.
1962   "Il numero dei fonemi in italiano in confronto con lo spagnolo", *LN* 23: 48-52.
Arthur, I.
1969-70 "Osservazioni sull'uso e sul non uso dell'articolo davanti ai nomi di isole e di gruppi insulari", *SNPh* 41: 253-97; 42: 105-56.
Ascoli, G. I.
1967   *Scritti sulla questione della lingua*, a cura di C. Grassi (Milano: Silva). [2nd revised edition: (Torino: Giappichelli 1968)]
Atti
1968   *Atti del convegno sul tema: "L'automazione elettronica e le sue implicazioni scientifiche, tecniche e sociali", svoltosi a Roma dal 16 al 19 ottobre 1967* (= *Problemi attuali di scienza e cultura; quaderno* 110) (Roma: Accademia Nazionale dei Lincei).
1969a   *La grammatica e la lessicologia; atti del 1 e del 2 convegno di studi* (Roma: Bulzoni). [27-28 May 1967 and 27-28 April 1968] [offset; typeset reprint: (1973)]
1969b   *La sintassi; atti del 3 convegno internazionale di studi* (Roma 17-18 maggio 1969) (Roma: Bulzoni).
1971a   *Grammatica trasformazionale italiana; atti del convegno internazionale di studi (Roma 29-30 novembre 1969)* (Roma: Bulzoni).
1971b   *L'insegnamento dell'italiano in Italia e all'estero; atti del quarto convegno internazionale di studi (Roma 1-2 giugno 1970)* (Roma: Bulzoni).
1973   *Storia linguistica dell'Italia nel Novecento; atti del 5 convegno internazionale di studi (Roma 1-2 giugno 1971)* (Roma: Bulzoni).
1974   *Fenomeni morfologici e sintattici nell'italiano contemporaneo; atti del 6 convegno internazionale di studi (Roma 4-6 settembre 1972)* (Roma: Bulzoni).

Baldelli, I.
1963   "Panorama dell'italiano novecentesco", *Rassegna della letteratura italiana* 67: 401-24. [reprinted as final chapter in Migliorini - Baldelli (1964: 315-347)].
1965   *Varianti di prosatori contemporanei (Palazzeschi, Cecchi, Bassani, Cassola, Testori)* (= *Bibliotechina del saggiatore* 21) (Firenze: Le Monnier).
1971   *Medioevo volgare da Montecassino all'Umbria* (Bari: Adriatica).
Bandini, F. - L. Polato - P. Spezzani - P. V. Mengaldo - A. M. Mutterle
1966   *Ricerche sulla lingua poetica contemporanea; Rebora, Saba, Ungaretti, Montale, Pavese*, presentazione di G. Folena (= *Quaderni del circolo filologico e linguistico padovano* 1) (Padova: Liviana).
Barbi, M. - G. Pasquali - G. Nencioni
1957   *Per un grande vocabolario storico della lingua italiana* (Firenze: Sansoni).
Barmeyer, E.
1886   "Die Nominalkomposition im Italienischen", *Programm des Johanneums zu Lüneburg, Ostern 1886* (Lüneburg): 3-14.
Bartoli, M.
1936   "Caratteri fondamentali della lingua nazionale italiana e delle lingue sorelle", in: *Miscellanea della facoltà di lettere e filosofia della regia Università di Torino* (Torino: Bona), pp. 69-106.
Bascetta, C.
1962   *Il linguaggio sportivo contemporaneo* (= *Biblioteca di Lingua nostra* 12) (Firenze: Sansoni).
1964   *Giornalismo e tipografia* (= *Glossari di lingua contemporanea* 1) (Roma: Armando).

50

Battacchi, M. W. - G. M. Facchini - A. Fassò - M. Montanini-Manfredi
1968-69 "Lo sviluppo dell'articolazione fonetica nei fanciulli: dai 2 anni e mezzo ai 4 anni", *Bollettino della Società italiana di fonetica, foniatria e audiologia* 17.

Battacchi, M. W. - G. M. Facchini - M. Montanini-Manfredi - Olivo Rubatta
1964 "Presentazione di un reattivo per l'esame dell'articolazione nei fanciulli in età prescolare di lingua italiana", *Bollettino della Società italiana di fonetica, foniatria e audiologia* 13: 441-86.

Battaglia, S.
1961- *Grande dizionario della lingua italiana* (Torino: Unione Tipografico - Editrice Torinese). [in progress: 8 vols. 1: *A-Balb* (1961) till 8: *Ini-Libb* (1973) published so far]

Battaglia, S. - V. Pernicone
1951 *La grammatica italiana* (Torino: Loescher). [2nd edition: (1954)]

Battisti, C.
1938 *Fonetica generale* (Milano: Hoepli).

Battisti, C. - G. Alessio
1950-57 *Dizionario etimologico italiano*, 5 vol. (Florence: Barbera). [1: *A-Ca* (1950); 2: *Ca-Fa* (1951); 3: *Fa-Me* (1952); 4: *Me-Ra* (1950); 5: *Ra-Zu* (1957)] [cf. Alessio (1957-58, 1962)]

Bausani, A. - G. R. Cardona
1970 "In margine al vol. 20 del 'Französisches etymologisches Wörterbuch' di W. v. Wartburg", *AION-O* 30: 121-32.

Beccaria, G. L.
1959 "L'unità melodica nella prosa italiana", *AGI* 44: 102-141.
1960 "Strutture melodiche nella prosa d'arte moderna", *LI* 12: 40-72.
1964 *Ritmo e melodia nella prosa italiana; studi e ricerche sulla prosa italiana* (Firenze: Olschki).
1968 *Spagnolo e Spagnoli in Italia; riflessi ispanici sulla lingua italiana del Cinque- e del Seicento* (= Università di Torino, pubblicazioni della facoltà di lettere e filosofia 19.1) (Torino: Giappichelli).

Beccaria, G.L. (ed.)
1973 *I linguaggi settoriali in Italia* (Milano: Bompiani).

Belgeri, L.
1929 *Les affriquées en italien et dans les autres principales langues européennes; étude de phonétique expérimentale* (Grenoble: chez l'auteur). [thèse de doctorat]

Berruto, G.
1971 "Per una semiologia dei rapporti tra lingua e dialetto", *Parole e metodi* 1: 45-58

Berruto, G. - D. Calleri - A. Sobrero
1972 "La linguistica applicata", *Parole e metodi* 3: 59-89. [Italian is treated best in par 13-18]

Bertoni, G.
1940 *Profilo linguistico d'Italia* (= Istituto di filologia romanza della Università di Roma, Testi e manuali 16) (Modena: Società tipografica modenese).

Bertoni, G. - F. A. Ugolini
1939a "L'asse linguistico Roma-Firenze", *LN* 1: 25-27
1939b *Prontuario di pronunzia e di ortografia* (Torino: EIAR = Ente Italiano per le Audizioni Radiofoniche).

Black, J. W. - M. Guirao
1955 "Notes on Italian vowels", in *Contributi del laboratorio di psicologia* 19 (= Pubblicazioni dell'Università Cattolica del S. Cuore, n.s. 49) (Milano: Vita e pensiero), pp. 67-70.

51

Blanc, L. G.
1844   *Grammatik der italienischen Sprache* (Halle: Schwetschke & Sohn).
Baragiola, A.
1880   *Italienische Grammatik mit Berücksichtigung des Lateinischen und der romanischen Schwestersprachen* (Strassburg: Trübner).
Bonfante, G.
1961   "Esiste il neutro in italiano?", *Quaderni dell'Istituto di Glottologia dell'Università di Bologna* 6: 103-110.
1964   "Il neutro in italiano, romeno e albanese", *Acta philologica* 3: 27-37.
1967   "La pronunzia dell'italiano", *ID* 30: 181-92.
Bonfante, G. - M.L. Porzio Gernia
1964   *Cenni di fonética e di fonemática con particolare riguardo all'italiano* (Torino: Giappichelli).
Borrani Castiglione, P.
1957   *Italian phonetics, diction and intonation* (New York: Vanni).
Bortolini, U. - C. Tagliavini - A. Zampolli
1972   *Lessico di frequenza della lingua italiana contemporanea* (Milano: Garzanti). [1st ed. (IBM Italia 1971), not for sale]
Bortolini, U. - A. Zampolli
1971   "Lessico di frequenza della lingua italiana contemporanea: prospettive metodologiche", in *Atti* (1971: 639-48).
Boström, I.
1972   *La morfosintassi dei pronomi personali soggetti della terza persona in italiano e fiorentino; contributo allo studio storico dei rapporti fra l'italiano standard e la varietà fiorentina* (Stockholm: Almqvist & Wiksell).
Braga, G.
1969   "Studio del comportamento delle comunità linguistiche dell'Alto Adige", in *Giornate* (1969: 353-67). [English translation, pp. 368-79]
Brambilla Ageno, F.
1964   *Il verbo nell'italiano antico; ricerche di sintassi* (Milano - Napoli: Ricciardi).
Brodin, G.
1970   *Termini dimostrativi toscani; studio storico di morfologia, sintassi e semantica* (= Etudes Romanes de Lund 19) (Lund: Gleerup).
Brøndal, R.
1941   "La signification du préfixe italien s-", *AL* 2: 151-64.
Bronzini, G. B.
1971   "Unità d'Italia: lingua nazionale e poesia popolare", *CultNeol* 31: 313-37
Brunet, J.
1971   *Cours de grammaire descriptive de l'italien (= Centre Universitaire Expérimental de Vincennes, Centre de Documentation Universitaire 5)* (Paris). [mimeographed]
Busa, R. - C. Croatto - L. Martinolli - L. Croatto - C. Tagliavini - A. Zampolli
1963   "Una ricerca statistica sulla composizione fonologica della lingua italiana parlata, eseguita con un sistema IBM a schede perforate", in *Proceedings of the 12th international speech and voice therapy conference* (Ed.: L. Croatto - C. Croatto Martinolli) (Padova: Scuola Tipografica dell'Ente Nazionale Sordomuti), pp. 542-62.
Calboli, G.
1970   "Costrittori nelle proposizioni complemento: i modi del verbo e l'infinito", in *Atti* (1970a: 63-96).
Camilli, A.
1909   "Gradi consonantici in italiano", *Classici e Neo-Latini* 5: 260-64.
1910   "Le nasali condizionate in italiano", *Le maître phonétique* 25: 44-5.

52

1911a   "Ancora dei rafforzamenti iniziali in italiano", *Le maître phonétique* 26: 72-4.
1911b   " 'i' e 'j' in italiano", *Le maître phonétique* 26: 75.
1913   "I rafforzamenti iniziali in italiano", *ASNS* 131: 170-4.
1921   *An Italian phonetic reader* (London: University of London Press).
1928   "Le vocali e, o in italiano", *Le maître phonétique* 43: 1-2. [= Camilli (1965: 71-3)]
1936   "Note di pronuncia italiana", *Italica* 13: 6.
1937   "Le vocali 'e', 'o' ", *Italica* 14: 117-25.
1938   "Lingua toscana in bocca romana", *Italica* 15: 55-6. [= Camilli (1965: 155-66)]
1941a   *Pronuncia e grafia dell'italiano* (Firenze: Sansoni). [2nd edition, revised (1947); 3rd edition, revised: Camilli (1965)]
1941b   "Intorno al problema degli accenti grafici", *LN* 3: 140-1.
1941c   "I rafforzamenti iniziali", *LN* 3: 44-5.
1950   "Spostamenti di tono nella pronuncia italiana", *LN* 11: 74.
1951   "La radio e la pronuncia", *LN* 12: 25-6.
1953a   "Per un sistema di accenti in italiano", *LN* 14: 91.
1953b   "Ancora della -s- tra vocali", *LN* 14: 31.
1955   "Ancora delle palatali sibilanti", *LN* 16: 85-7.
1956   "Il ritmo intensivo italiano", *LN* 17: 26. [= Camilli(1965: 269-75)]
1959   *I fondamenti della prosodia italiana* (Firenze: Circolo Linguistico Fiorentino). [= Camilli (1965: 243-279)]
1965   *Pronuncia e grafia dell'italiano* (= *Biblioteca di lingua nostra* 2) (Florence: Sansoni). [= 3rd edition, revised by P. Fiorelli, of Camilli (1941a)]

Cantagalli, R.
1972   *Con rispetto parlando. Semantica del doppio senso* (Milano: Sugar).
Cappuccini, G.
1916   *Vocabolario della lingua italiana* (Torino: Paravia).
Cappuccini, R. - B. Migliorini
1945   *Vocabolario della lingua italiana* (Torino: Paravia). [cf. Migliorini (1965)].
Caramella, S.
1967   *Pedagogia. Saggio di voci nuove* (= *Glossari di lingua contemporanea* 6) (Roma: Armando).
Cardona, G. R.
1969a   *Linguistica generale* (= *Glossari di lingua contemporanea* 10) (Roma: Armando).
1969b   "Bibliografia degli scritti di Antonino Pagliaro", in *Studia Classica et Orientalia Antonino Pagliaro oblata* III (Roma: Istituto di Glottologia), pp. 311-324.
1973a   "L'elemento di origine o di trafila portoghese nella lingua dei viaggiatori italiani del '500", *BALM* 14. [to appear]
1973b   Review of Pellegrini (1972), *LN* 34: 29-31.
1974   *La lingua della pubblicità* (Ravenna: Longo).
Carlà, M.
1967   *Cibernetica e teoria dell'informazione* (= *Glossari di lingua contemporanea* 7) (Roma: Armando).
Carlsson, L.
1966   *Le degré de cohésion des groupes "subst. + de + subst." en français contemporain étudié d'après la place accordée à l'adjectif épithète. Avec examen comparatif des groupes correspondants de l'italien et de l'espagnol* (= *Acta Universitatis Upsaliensis; Studia Romanica Upsaliensia* 3) (Uppsala: Almqvist & Wiksell)
1969   *Le type "C'est le meilleur livre qu'il ait jamais écrit" en espagnol, en italien et en français* (= *Acta Universitatis Upsaliensis; Studia Romanica Upsaliensia* 5) (Uppsala: Almqvist & Wiksell)

Casagrande, G.
1967   "Modern usage and syntactic construction of the impersonal *si* in Italian", *MLJ* 51: 492-96.
Casilli, A.
1969   "Basi formali del congiuntivo in italiano", in *Atti* (1969a: 163-65).
Castagnotto, U.
1970   *Semantica della pubblicità* (Roma: Silva).
Castelfranchi, C.
1971   "Capacità locative e aspetti dei tempi verbali", in *Atti* (1971b: 649-65).
Castelfranchi, C. - D. Parisi
1969   "Analisi semantica dei locativi spaziali", in *Atti* (1969a: 193-217).
Castellani, A.
1954   "*Gl* intervocalico in italiano", *LN* 15: 66-70.
1956   "Fonemi e fonotipi in italiano", *SFI* 14: 435-453.
1960   "Il nesso 'si' in italiano", *SLI* 1: 49-70, 174-175.
1961-65 "Sulla formazione del tipo fonetico italiano", *SLI* 2: 24-45; 5: 89-96.
1962a   "Proposte ortogràfiche", *SLI* 3: 188-91.
1962b   "La diphtongaison des *e* et *o* ouverts en italien", in: *Linguistique et philologie romanes; 10e Congrès international de linguistique et philologie romanes,* [...]Strasbourg du 23 au 28 avril 1962, *Actes* (Ed.: G. Straka) (*Actes et colloques* 4) (Paris: Klincksieck 1965), pp. 951-964.
Cernecca, D.
1962   "Un tipo di costruzione assoluta dell'italiano moderno", *SRAZ* 13-14: 85-108.
1963   "L'inversione del soggetto nella frase dei 'Promessi sposi' ", *SRAZ* 15-16: 49-98.
1965   "Struttura della frase e inversione del soggetto nella prosa della 'Vita Nuova' ", *SRAZ* 19-20: 137-160.
1966   "Una caratteristica contaminazione di costrutti sintattici", *SRAZ* 21-22: 89-101.
1968   "Prosa e poesia e inversione del soggetto nella frase del 'Convivio' ", *SRAZ* 25-26: 43-67.
1972   "Costruzione diretta e costruzione inversa della frase indipendente", in *Scritti* (1972: 79-90).
Chapallaz, M.
1960   "Notes on Italian intonation", *Le maître phonétique* 3.38 (= 75): 10-13.
1962   "Further notes on Italian intonation", *Le maître phonétique* 3.40 (= 77): 5-7.
1964   "Notes on the intonation of questions in Italian", in: *In honour of Daniel Jones; papers contributed on the occasion of his eightieth birthday, 12 September 1961* (Ed.: D. Abercrombie - D. B. Fry - P. A. D. MacCarthy - N. C. Scott - J. L. M. Trim) (London: Longmans), pp. 306-12.
Chiappelli, F.
1954   "Note sul tipo 'mi lavo le mani' ", *LN* 15: 56-59.
Chomsky, N.
o1965   *Aspects of the theory of syntax* (Cambridge, Mass.: M.I.T. Press).
Chomsky, N. - M. Halle
o1968   *The sound pattern of English* (New York: Harper & Row).
Cinque, G.
1972   "Analisi componenziale e del lessico: prospettiva per una applicazione contrastiva", in *Scritti* (1972: 93-108).
Cîrstea, M.
1972   "La generazione di alcuni costrutti enfatici nell'italiano contemporaneo", in *Scritti* (1972: 121-37).

1972   "Costrutto perifrastico con valore aspettuale nell'italiano contemporaneo",
            in *Scritti* (1972: 141-57).
Clivio, G. P.
1968   "A note on two oppositions of Standard Italian with a low functional
            yield", in: *Studies presented to Professor Roman Jakobson by his students*
            (Ed.: Ch. E. Gribble) (Cambridge, Mass.: Slavica Publishers), pp. 70-75.
1972   "La struttura della proposizione semplice indipendente in italiano e in
            inglese: problemi didattici in chiave contrastiva", in *Scritti* (1972: 109-
            117).
Colombo, A.
1969   "I determinanti in italiano: un esperimento di grammatica generativa",
            LeS 4: 183-203.
1971   "Appunti per una grammatica delle proposizioni completive", in *Atti*
            (1971a: 134-161).
Consiglio, C.
1946   "Del plural italiano de los nombres compuestos y de algunas cuestiones
            filológicas inherentes al mismo", *Boletín de la Biblioteca Menéndez y
            Pelayo* 22: 236-54.
Conte, M. -E.
1972   "Vocativo ed imperativo secondo il modello performativo", in *Scritti*
            (1972: 161-79).
Contreras, H.
1962-63   "Una clasificación morfo-sintáctica de las lenguas románicas", *RPh* 16:
            261-8.
Cordié, C.
1963a   "Cuce meglio", *LN* 24: 65-7.
1963b   "Va-sano", *LN* 24: 90.
1963c   "Autodemolizione", *LN* 24: 22.
Cortelazzo, M.
1969-72   *Avviamento critico allo studio della dialettologia italiana* (Pisa: Pacini).
            [1: *Problemi e metodi;* 3: *Lineamenti d'italiano popolare*]
1970   *L'influsso linguistico greco a Venezia* (= *Linguistica* 2) (Bologna: Pàtron).
1973   "Lingua pubblicitaria e italiano comune", *SIPRA* 4 (July-August): 15-19.
Costabile, N.
1967   *Le strutture della lingua italiana; grammatica generativo-trasformativa*
            (Bologna: Pàtron).
1969   "La flessione verbale italiana", in *Atti* (1969: 219-260).
1972   "L'assegnazione dell'accento tonico in italiano", in *Scritti* (1972: 183-211).
Court, C.
1967   "On /s/ and /z/ in Standard Italian", *Lingua* 18: 290-5.
Còveri, L.
1973   "I contributi italiani alla sociolinguistica. Rassegna bibliografica", *SILTA*
            2: 475-95.
Crisari, M.
1969   "Un'interpretazione fonetica: [v]", in *Atti* (1969a: 167-174).
1971   "Le preposizioni semplici italiane: un approccio semantico", in *Atti* (1971a:
            97-116).
Crisari, M. - W. D'Addio
1967   "Caratteristiche prosodiche dell'italiano", *Homo loquens* 1: 3-23.
Crisari, M. - D. Parisi - A. Puglielli
1971   "Le congiunzioni temporali, spaziali e causali in italiano", in *Atti* (1971a:
            117-134).
Croatto, L. - M. Accordi - C. Croatto - G. P. Feltrin - E. Magno Caldognetto
1971   "Studio roentgencinematografico con sincrona analisi elettroacustica del
            messaggio verbale della lingua italiana", in: *Atti del XI Congresso Nazionale*

55

della Società italiana di audiologia e foniatria (Torino), pp. 10-43.
Crocetti, L.
1961   *Indici di "Lingua Nostra" 1939-1959* (Firenze: Sansoni).

D'Addio, W.
1969a   "Su alcune modalità di suffissazione in italiano", in *Atti* (1969a: 117-25).
1969b   "Per una sintassi della derivazione in italiano", in *Atti* (1969b: 261-92).
1971   "Suffissi derivativi aggettivali dell'italiano: analisi semantica", in *Atti* (1971a: 163-75).
Dalbiac, Ph. H. - Th. B. Harbottle (comp.)
°1901   *Dictionary of quotations (French and Italian)* (= *Sonnenschein's dictionaries of quotations* 3) (London: Sonnenschein & Co.; New York: MacMillan).
Dardano, M.
1968   "La sintassi dell'italiano contemporaneo", *Ulisse* (Firenze) 21: 49-59.
1969a   *Lingua e tecnica narrativa nel Duecento* (= *Biblioteca di cultura* 3) (Roma: Bulzoni).
1969b   "Aspetti sintattici della lingua dei giornali", in *Atti* (1969b: 293-305).
1973a   "Questioni di metodo nello studio della lingua dei giornali", in *Atti* (1973: 15-38).
1973b   *Il linguaggio dei giornali italiani* (Bari: Laterza).
D'Aronco, G.
1952a   "Nitratate! ", *LN* 13: 93.
1952b   "Verbi in *-izzare* da nomi di persona", *LN* 13: 93.
Davis, E. B.
1937   "Italian e's and o's", *Italica* 14: 117-25.
De Boer, C.
1926   *Essai sur la syntaxe moderne de la préposition en français et en italien* (Paris: Champion).
Deferrari, H. A.
1954   *The phonology of Italian, Spanish, and French* (Ann Arbor: Edward Brothers). [Italian, pp. 123-233]
De Gregorio, G.
1932   "Scoperta della genesi fisiologica delle cosiddette consonanti doppie", *Studi glottologici italiani* 9: 3-15.
1935   "La genesi delle così dette consonanti doppie o geminate", in *Atti del 3 congresso internazionale dei linguisti (Roma, 19-26 settembre 1933)* (Ed.: B. Migliorini - V. Pisani) (Firenze: Le Monnier), pp. 66-72.
De Mauro, T.
1963   *Storia linguistica dell'Italia unita* (Bari: Laterza). [2nd revised edition (1970)] [rec.: Hall (1964d)]
1968   "Lingua parlata e TV", in: *Televisione e vita italiana* (Torino: Edizioni Rai), pp. 247-294. [= De Mauro (1970: 430-58)]
1970   "Per lo studio dell'italiano popolare unitario", in A. Rossi, *Lettere di una tarantata* (Bari: De Donato), pp. 43-75.
Denison, N.
1969   "Sociolinguistic aspects of plurilingualism", in *Giornate* (1969: 255-78).
Devoto, G.
1939   "Il prefisso *s-* in italiano", in: *Mélanges de linguistique offerts à Charles Bally* (Genève: Georg Droz), pp. 263-9. [= Devoto (1972: 30-35)]
1940   "L' "aspetto" del verbo", *LN* 2: 35-38. [= Devoto (1972: 9-15)]
1953   *Profilo di storia linguistica italiana* (Florence: La Nuova Italia). [2nd edition "con note bibliografiche e critiche" 1954; 1960³, 1964⁴]
1966   *Avviamento alla etimologia italiana; dizionario etimologico* (Firenze: Le Monnier). [2nd revised edition: (1968)]
1972   *Scritti minori* 3 (Firenze: Le Monnier).

56

Devoto, G. - M. L. Altieri
1968   La lingua italiana; storia e problemi attuali (Torino: Edizioni Rai Radio-
           televisione italiana).
Devoto, G. - B. Migliorini - A. Schiaffini
1962   Cento anni di lingua italiana (1861-1961) (Milano: Scheiwiller).
Devoto, G. - G. C. Oli
1967   Vocabolario illustrato della lingua italiana, 2 vol. (Milano: Selezione del
           Reader's Digest. [compact edition in one volume: Firenze: Le Monnier
           1967); 2nd edition, slightly abridged: Devoto - Oli (1971)]
1971   Dizionario della lingua italiana (Firenze: Le Monnier). [concise one-
           volume edition of Devoto - Oli (1967)]
Di Luzio, A.
1967   Review of Regula - Jernej (1965), ASNSP 204: 223-28.
Di Maria, F.
1969   "Atteggiamento politico e differenziale semantico", in Giornate (1969:
           459-71). [English translation, pp. 472-83]
Di Pietro, R. J.
1965   "The phonemic status of juncture in Italian", in: Proceedings of the
           fifth International Congress of Phonetic Sciences (Ed.: E. Zwirner)
           (Basel: Karger), pp. 261-63.
1967   "Phonemics, generative grammar and the Italian sibilants", SL 21:
           96-106.
1970   Review of Muljačić (1969), Lg 46: 705-12.
1971a   Language structures in contrast (Rowley Mass.: Newbury House).
1971b   Review of Saltarelli (1970a), Lg 47: 718-30.
Dizionario
1937   Dizionario di marina medioevale e moderno, a cura di G. Bertoni,
           E. Falqui, A. Prati (Roma: Reale Accademia d'Italia).
D'Ovidio, F. - W. Meyer-Lübke
1888   "Die italienische Sprache", in: Grundriss der romanischen Philologie
           (Ed.: G. Gröber) (Strassburg: Trübner), pp. 489-560. [2nd edition:
           (1904: 637-711)]
1906   Grammatica storica della lingua e dei dialetti italiani, tradotta per
           cura del dottore E. Polcari (Milano: Hoepli). [1919², 1932³]
Durante, M.
1962   "Desinenze verbali italiane", BCSS 6 (= Saggi e ricerche in memoria
           di E. Li Gotti 1): 515-23.
1970   "I pronomi personali nell'italiano contemporaneo", BCSS 11: 180-
           202.
Duro, A.
1966a   "La rinnovata attività lessicografica dell'Accademia della Crusca",
           SFI 24: 609-29.
1966b   "Les nouvelles méthodes du Dictionnaire historique de la langue
           italienne", Clex 8: 95-111.
1967a   "Notizie sul Vocabolario", SFI 25: 315-21. [cf. Duro (1970)]
1967b   "Elaborazione elettronica di dati linguistici, Cultura e scuola
           23: 7-15.
1968   "Humanities computing activities in Italy", Computers and the
           Humanities 3: 49-52.
1969   "Notizie sul vocabolario", SFI 27: 255-63. [cf. Duro (1970)]
1970   "Notizie sul vocabolario", SFI 28: 399-406. [Duro (1967a, 1969,
           1970) include lists of texts punched so far.]
1971   "Panorama della lessicologia e della lessicografia italiane negli ultimi
           trent'anni", in Atti (1971: 667-74).

Duro, A. - A. Zampolli
1968   "Analisi lessicali mediante elaboratori elettronici, in *Atti* (1968: 119-
        139).

Ebneter, Th.
1972   "L'incastro della proposizione soggetto in italiano in confronto col
        francese", *Studi italiani di linguistica teorica e applicata* 1: 69-84.

Enciclopedia
1955-61 *Dizionario enciclopedico italiano*, 12 vol. (Roma: Istituto dell'Enci-
         clopedia Italiana). [a further volume was published in 1969, with new
         entries and corrections to older ones]
1970-   *Enciclopedia dantesca*, directed by U. Bosco and G. Petrocchi (Roma:
         Istituto dell'Enciclopedia Italiana). [Four volumes published so far; *A-Sam.*]

Fanfani, P.
1855   *Vocabolario della lingua italiana* (Firenze: Le Monnier).[1865^2, 1891^3]

Fanfani, P. - C. Arlìa
1877   *Il lessico della corrotta italianità* (Milano: Carrara). [from 1881 further
        editions had the title: *Lessico dell'infima e corrotta italianità*]

Ferrero, E.
1972   *I gerghi della malavita dal Cinquecento a oggi* (Milano: Mondadori).

Ferrero, F.E.
1968   "Diagrammi di esistenza delle vocali italiane", *Alta frequenza* 37: 54-
        58.
1972   "Caratteristiche acustiche dei fonemi vocalici italiani", *Parole e metodi*
        3: 9-31.

Ferrero, F. E. - U. Stålhammar
1972   "A preliminary study on the acoustic characteristics of the Italian vowels
        in some dysillabic constructs", *Quarterly progress and status report of the
        speech transmission laboratory, Stockholm* 2-3

Fiorelli, P.
1947   "Per un vocabolario giuridico italiano", *LN* 8: 96-108. [cf. above *5.2.3.2*]
1951   "Una sibilante e due campane", *LN* 12: 81-86.
1952   "Senso e premesse d'una fonetica fiorentina", *LN* 13: 57-63.
1955   "Le palatoalveolari come fonemi", *LN* 16: 85-87.
1958   "Del raddoppiamento da parola a parola", *LN* 19: 122-27.
1964   *Córso di pronùnzia italiana* (Padova: Rádar). [with 14 7" rpm records]

Fochi, F.
1953   "I verbi in -*ionare*", *LN* 14: 84-89.
1964   *L'italiano facile* (Milano: Feltrinelli).
1966   *Lingua in rivoluzione* (Milano: Feltrinelli).

Fogarasi, M.
1969   *Grammatica italiana del Novecento. Sistemazione descrittiva* (Budapest:
        Tankönyvkiadó)

Folena, G.
1958   Review of Rüegg (1956), *LN* 19: 132-35.
1964   "Aspetti della lingua contemporanea; la lingua e la pubblicità", *Cultura e
        scuola* 3: 53-62.

Fornaciari, R.
1879   *Grammatica italiana dell'uso moderno* (Firenze: Sansoni). [7th edition:
        (1934)]
1881   *Sintassi italiana dell'uso moderno* (Firenze: Sansoni). [With corrections: 1897;
        reprint 1974, introduction: G. Nencioni.]

Foster, D. W.
1968   "A survey of development of Latin *ĕ* and *ŏ* in Italian in relation to con-
        sonantal gemination", *Orbis* 17: 399-407.

58

Fracastoro Martini, O.
1951   *La lingua e la radio* (= *Biblioteca di lingua nostra* 9) (Florence: Sansoni).
Francescato, G.
1954   "L'adattamento fonetico dei bilingui italiani in Danimarca", *LN* 15: 118-21.
1961   "Systèmes coexistants ou systèmes diachroniques", *Neophilologus* 45: 37-44.
1968   Review of Regula - Jernej (1965), *ZRPh* 84: 271-77.
1970   *Il linguaggio infantile. Strutturazione e apprendimento* (Torino: Einaudi).
1971   "Nudo, spoglio, scoperto. Una esercitazione di polisemia differenziale", in: *Interlinguistica - Sprachvergleich und Übersetzung; Festschrift zum 60. Geburtstag von Mario Wandruszka* (Ed.: K. R. Bausch - H. M. Gauger) (Tübingen: Niemeyer), pp. 115-22.
Franceschi, T.
1964   "La scrittura dello zeta e la struttura fonematica dell'italiano", *BALI* 9-10: 36-50.
1965   *Sulla pronunzia di* e, o, s, z *nelle parole di non diretta tradizione con cenni sulla lenizione consonantica e la dittongazione in Toscana* (Torino: Giappichelli). [rec.: Valesio (1967d)]
Frontali, A.
1943-44 "Lo sviluppo del linguaggio articolato nel bambino", *VR* 7: 214-43.
1962   "I problemi del linguaggio", *Quaderni dell'Accademia Nazionale dei Lincei* (Roma) 41: 95 seqq.
Fucilla, J. G.
1949   *Our Italian surnames* (Evanston, Ill.: Chandler).
1963   "New surnames in the making in Italy", *Orbis* 12: 456-62.
Gáldi, L.
1971   *Introduzione alla stilistica italiana* (= *Linguistica* 5) (Bologna: Pàtron).
Galli de' Paratesi, N.
1964   *Semantica dell'eufemismo. L'eufemismo e la repressione verbale con esempi tratti dall'italiano contemporaneo* (Torino: Giappichelli). [unchanged reprint: *Le brutte parole. Semantica dell'eufemismo* (Milano: Mondadori 1969)]
Garavelli Mortara, B.
1971   "Fra norma e invenzione: lo stile nominale", in *Studi* (1971: 71-316). [see below, Mortara]
Garde, P.
1968   *L'accent* (Paris: Presses Universitaires de France).
Gemelli, A. - G. Pastori
1934   *L'analisi elettroacustica del linguaggio* 2 vol. (= *Pubblicazioni dell'Università Cattolica del Sacro Cuore* 6.7) (Milano: Vita e Pensiero). [1: *Testo*; 2: *Tavole*]
Gerber de Boer, M.
1972   "Il problema dell'enfasi", in *Scritti* (1972: 69-78).
Gherardini, G.
1843   *Lessigrafia italiana o sia maniera di scrivere le parole italiane proposta e messa a confronto con quella insegnata dal Vocabolario della Crusca* (Milano: Bianchi).
1838-40 *Voci e maniere di dire italiane additate a' futuri vocabolaristi*, 2 vol. (Milano: Bianchi).
1852-57 *Supplimento a' Vocabolari italiani*, 5 vol. [1: *A-B* (Milano: Carlo Branca 1852); 2: *C-E* (Milano: Carlo Branca 1853); 3: *F-K* (Milano: P. A. Molina 1854); 4: *L-P* (Milano: G. Bernardoni 1855); 5: *Q-S* (Milano: P. A. Molina 1857)]

Giacomelli, R.
1954   "Le palatali sibilanti italiane e la loro trascrizione fonetica", *LN* 15: 176-84.

Giornate
1969   *Giornate internazionali di sociolinguistica, Roma 15-17 settembre 1969;* *secondo congresso internazionale di scienze sociali dell'Istituto Luigi Sturzo* (Roma: Tipografia V. Ferri).

Giovannelli, P.
1967   *Grund- und Aufbauwortschatz: Italienisch* (Stuttgart: Klett).

Giurescu, A.
1965   "Contributi al modo di definire i sostantivi composti della lingua italiana", *RRLing* 10: 395-400.
1967   "Continuité et discontinuité morphématiques appliquées aux substantifs de la langue italienne contemporaine standard", in Rosetti (1970: 615-620).
1968   "I composti italiani del tipo verbo-nome, risultati di una trasformazione di frase", *RRL* 13: 421-6.
1972   "Osservazioni su un tipo di gruppo nominale dell'italiano contemporaneo", in *Scritti* (1972: 215-9).

Goidànich, P. G.
1893   *La gutturale e la palatina nei plurali dei nomi toscani della prima e della seconda declinazione* (Salerno: Jovane).
1910   "Per la fisiologia delle rattratte *ć č z* ", in: *Miscellanea di studî in onore di Attilio Hortis* (Trieste: Caprin), pp. 929-45. [= Goidànich (1940: 254-64)]
1918   *Grammatica italianá* (Bologna: Zanichelli). [4th posthumous edition, with additions by the author and a new preface by L. Heilmann: (Bologna: Zanichelli, 1962)]
1925   *Le alterazioni fonetiche del linguaggio e le loro cause*(Bologna: Neri). [= Goidànich (1940: 55-102)]
1940   *Saggi linguistici* (Modena: Società Tipografica). [cf. Goidànich (1910, 1925)]

Gonnelli, P.
1966   *Cinema, teatro, televisione* (= *Glossari di lingua contemporanea* 4) (Roma: Armando).

Gossen, C. Th.
1954   *Studien zur syntaktischen und stilistischen Hervorhebung im modernen Italienischen* (= *Deutsche Akademie der Wissenschaften zu Berlin, Veröffentlichungen des Instituts für romanische Sprachwissenschaft* 12) (Berlin: Akademie Verlag).
1956   "Remarques sur l'emploi et la valeur des exclamations et des interjections invocatoires en italien", *RLR* 20: 268-308.
1963   " 'Rhetorisches' in der modernen italienischen Prosa: die Frage als Stilmittel", in: *Weltoffene Romanistik; Festschrift Alwin Kuhn* (Ed.: G. Plangg - E. Tiefenthaler) (= *Innsbrucker Beiträge zur Kulturwissenschaft* 9-10) (Innsbruck: Sprachwissenschaftliches Institut), pp. 111-20.

Grand, C.
1930   *Tu, Voi, Lei: étude des pronoms allocutoires en italien* (Ingenbohl: Théodose). [thèse Fribourg]

Grandgent, C. H.
1927   *From Latin to Italian. An historical outline of the phonology and morphology of the Italian language* (Cambridge: Harvard University Press). [3rd edition: ‥ (1940)]

Grassi, C.
1958   Review of Rüegg (1956), *RJb* 8: 228-33.
1964   "Comportamento linguistico e comportamento sociologico (A proposito di una recente pubblicazione)", *AGI* 49: 40-66.

1965a   *Corso di storia della lingua italiana*, a cura di E. Cane, T. Omézzoli, S. Quirino in 2 parti. (Torino: Giappichelli). [1: *Elementi di dialettologia italiana*; 2: *Lingua e dialetto, letteratura contemporanea (Italia meridionale e Roma)*]

1965b   "Ancora su 'Comportamento linguistico e comportamento sociologico' ", *AGI* 50: 1-10.

Griffith, T. G.

1967   *Italian writers and the "Italian" language* (Hull: University of Hull publications).

Guberina, P.

1958   "Etude expérimentale de l'expression linguistique", *SRAZ* 5: 33-50.

1959   "Le son et le mouvement dans le langage", *SRAZ* 7: 3-15.

Guiraud, P.

°1967   *Structures étymologiques du lexique français* (Paris: Larousse).

Guryčeva, M. S.

1966   *Sravnitel'no-sopostavitel'naja grammatika romanskix jazykov. Italoromanskaja podgruppa* [Comparative and contrastive grammar of Romance languages; Italo-Romance subgrouping] (Moskva: Nauka).

Guṭia, I.

1953   "Sull'uso della preposizione *con* nella prosa italiana contemporanea", *LN* 14: 13-19.

1958   "La negazione di parola nella prosa italiana contemporanea", *Orbis* 7:482-91.

Hall, A. H. Jr.

1942   *The Italian "questione della lingua"; an interpretative essay* (= *UNCSRLL* 4) (Chapel Hill, N. C.: [*s.e.*])

1944   'Italian phonemes and orthography", *Italica* 21: 72-82.

1947   "Latin -*s*- in Italian", *Lg* 23: 426-29.

1948   *Descriptive Italian grammar* (Ithaca, N. Y.: Cornell University Press - Linguistic Society of America)

1956   "Il plurale italiano in -*a*: un duale mancato? ", *Italica* 33: 140-42.

1958a   *Bibliografia della linguistica italiana*, 3 vols. [= 4 parts] (= *Biblioteca bibliografica italiana* 13-15) (Florence: Sansoni). [2nd revised edition; 1.1: *Storia della lingua*; 2: *Descrizione della lingua italiana*; 2[= 3]: *Dialettologia italiana*; 3[= 4]: *Storia della linguistica italiana; indici*; .- cf. *Primo supplemento decennale (1956-1966)* (= *Biblioteca bibliografica italiana* 35) (Firenze: Sansoni 1969)]

1958b   "Statistica sintattica: l'accordo del participio passato coniugato con 'avere'", *LN* 19: 95-100.

1959   "Moot points in Italian grammar 1: 'Preposizioni articolate' ", *Italica* 36: 56-59.

1960a   "Moot points in Italian grammar 2: 'Ventuna lira' o 'ventun(o) lire'? ", *Italica* 37: 163-66.

1960b   "Italian [z] and the converse of the archiphoneme", *Lingua* 9: 194-97.

1960c   "Statistica grammaticale: l'uso di 'gli', 'le' e 'loro' come regime indiretto", *LN* 21: 58-65.

1961   *Applied linguistics: Italian; a guide for teachers* (Boston: Heath).

1964a   *Italian for modern living* (Philadelphia: Chilton).

1964b   "Moot points in Italian grammar 3: Definite article + family name (masc.)", *Italica* 41: 162-67.

1964c   "Initial consonants and syntactic doubling in West Romance", *Lg* 40: 551-56.

1964d   Review of De Mauro (1963), *Lg* 40: 91-96.

1967a   Review of Migliorini - Griffith (1966), *Lg* 43: 974-77.

1967b   "The Italian sibilants again", *IRAL* 5: 211-13.

1971a   *La struttura dell'italiano* (Roma: Armando).
1971b   "The syllable in Italian phonology", *Linguistics* 67: 26-33.
1973   *Bibliografia essenziale della linguistica italiana e romanza* (Firenze: Sansoni). [Abridged and updated edition of Hall (1958a).]
Hall, R. A. jr. - C. Bartoli
1963   *Basic conversational Italian* (New York: Holt, Rinehart & Winston).
Hames, H. jr.
1969   "Italian intonation patterns in conversation and reading", *LeS* 4: 43-52.
Hamp, E. P.
1960   "Florentine stops", *Italica* 37: 126.
Hatcher, A. G. - M. Musa
1970   "On a certain pattern of the expanded verbal form in Italian", *La linguistique* 6: 51-64.
Heinimann, S.
1949   "Die italienischen Imperativkomposita", *ASNS* 186: 136-53.
Herczeg, G.
1954   "Stile nominale nella prosa italiana contemporanea", *ALH* 4: 171-92.
1955   "Complementi avverbiali in funzione determinativa", *LN* 16: 58-62.
1957   "L'apposizione in funzione di reggente di proposizioni subordinate", *LN* 18: 17-22.
1959a   "Un uso particolare della preposizione *con* nella prosa contemporanea", *LN* 20: 14-7.
1959b   "Sintassi delle proposizioni subordinate nella lingua italiana. Studio di grammatica descrittiva", *ALH* 9: 261-333.
1962a   "Proposizioni subordinate apparentemente ellittiche", in: *Romania; scritti offerti a Francesco Piccolo nel suo 70 compleanno* Napoli: Armanno), pp. 309-20.
1962b   "Su alcuni usi del presente", *LN* 23: 104-9.
1963a   *Lo stile indiretto libero in italiano* (= *Biblioteca di Lingua nostra* 13) (Firenze : Sansoni).
1963b   "Le enumerazioni appositive nella prosa moderna", *LN* 24: 49-56.
1964   "Collegamento copulativo tra proposizioni subordinate", *LN* 25: 95-101.
1965   "Infinito descrittivo e narrativo in italiano", *RCCM* 7: 561-76.
1966   "La locuzione perifrastica '*andare* + participio passato' ", *LN* 27: 58-64.
1967   *Lo stile nominale in italiano* (= *Bibliotechina del saggiatore* 25) (Firenze: Le Monnier).
1969   "Il 'futuro nel passato' in italiano", *LN* 30: 63-68.
1970   *Olasz leíró nyelvtan* [Descriptive Italian grammar] (Budapest: Terra).
1972a   *Studi linguistici e stilistici* (= *Accademia Toscana di scienze e lettere "La Colombaria", studi* 24) (Firenze: Olschki).
1972b   "Congiuntivo e ipotassi", *LN* 33: 14-19. [Review article of Schmitt-Jensen (1970)]
Hijmans-Tromp, I.
1964   *Italiaanse grammatica*, met medewerking van Mario L. Alinei (Arnhem: van Loghum Slaterus).
Hope, T. E.
1971   *Lexical borrowing in the Romance languages; a critical study of Italianisms in French and of Gallicisms in Italian from 1100 to 1900* (Oxford: Oxford University Press)
Huber-Sauter, M.
1951   *Zur Syntax des Imperativs im Italienischen* (= *Romanica Helvetica* 36) (Bern: Francke).
Jeremić, T.
1969   "Le esercitazioni ortoepiche, ortografiche, morfologiche e lessicali di italiano con l'aiuto del registratore", *RILA* 1: 53-61.

62

Jernej, J.
1961   "Intorno alla classificazione delle preposizioni indipendenti secondo il loro contenuto", *SRAZ* 11: 21-28.
1966   "I complementi nominali della frase", *SRAZ* 21-22: 77-87.
1967   "Tassemi e sintagmi", *SRAZ* 23: 81-85.
Jones, D. - A. Camilli
1933   *Fondamenti di grafia fonetica secondo il sistema dell'Associazione fonetica internazionale* (= *Le maître phonétique, supplément*) (Hertford: International Phonetic Association).
Josselyn, F. M.
1899a   "De la nasalité en italien", *La parole* 9: 602-10.
1899b   "Note sur *i* et *u* consonnes, *c(e)* et *g(e)* en italien", *La parole* 9: 933-44.
1901   *Etudes expérimentales de phonétique italienne* (Paris: La Parole).
1904   "Nasality in Italian", *MLN* 19: 254-55.
Junker, A.
1955   *Wachstum und Wandlungen im neuesten italienischen Wortschatz* (= *Erlanger Forschungen* A 2) (Erlangen: Universitätsbund).
1957   "Gesunkenes Metapherngut im zeitgenössischen Italienischen", in: *Syntactica und Stilistica; Festschrift für Ernst Gamillscheg zum 70. Geburtstag, 20. Oktober 1957* (Ed.: G. Reichenkron) (Tübingen: Niemeyer), pp. 243-59.
1958   "Allerneueste Präfixbildungen im Italienischen", in: *Romanica. Festschrift für Gerhard Rohlfs* (Ed.: H. Lausberg - H. Weinrich) (Halle: Niemeyer), pp. 216-30.

Kässmayer-Beran, B.
1965   *Die asyndetische Konstruktion in der modernen italienischen Prosa* (Wien). [dissertation; typescript]
Karulin, Ju. A.
1960   "Prigagol'nyj infinitiv v sovremennom ital'janskom jazyke" [Adverbal infinitive in contemporary Italian], *Voprosy jazyka i literatury* 2: 28-35.
Klajn, I.
1967   "I nessi consonantici dell'italiano", *LN* 28: 74-81.
1972   *Influssi inglesi nella lingua italiana* (= *Accademia Toscana di scienze e lettere "La colombaria", studi* 22) (Firenze: Olschki). [= Italian version of Klajn's doctoral dissertation: *Uticaji engleskog jazyka u književnom italjianskom jeziku* (Beograd 1970)]
Koning, W.
1941   "Aveva i capelli biondi", *RF* 56: 410-12.
Krámský, J.
1964   "A quantitative phonemic analysis of Italian mono-, di- and trisyllabic words", *TLP* 1: 129-43.
Krenn, H.
1966   *Die sprachwissenschaftliche Frage der Semantik und Funktion erläutert an den Gegebenheiten der consecutio temporum im Italienischen* (Frankfurt am Main). [doctoral dissertation; mimeographed]
1970   "L'aggettivo in italiano: un problema di grammatica generativa", in Rosetti (1970: 505-510).
1971   "Per un'analisi generativa dell'enfasi in italiano", in *Atti* (1971: 177-90).
1972   "Critica dell'indipendenza della proposizione semplice indipendente", in *Scritti* (1972: 223-31).
Kristeller, P. O.
1946   "The origin and development of the language of Italian prose", *Word* 2: 50-65. [reprinted in [his] *Studies in Renaissance thought and letters* (Roma: Edizioni di Storia e Letteratura 1956), pp. 473-93; Italian translation: "L'o-

rigine e lo sviluppo della prosa volgare italiana", *CultNeol* 10(1950): 137-56]

Labande-Jeanroy, Th.
1925   *La question de la langue en Italie* (Paris: Presses Universitaires de France). [Faculté des Lettres de l'Université de Strasbourg, doctoral dissertation]

Lausberg, H.
1947   "Vergleichende Charakteristik der italienischen und der spanischen Schriftsprache", *RF* 60: 106-22.
1948   "Beiträge zur italienischen Lautlehre. 1: Zum Vokalismus, 2: Zum Konsonantismus, 3: Zur Stellung Italiens in der Romania", *RF* 61: 300-23.
1956   *Romanische Sprachwissenschaft* 2 vol. (Berlin: Göschen). [2nd edition: (1963-67); Italian translation: *Linguistica romanza*, translated by A. Pasera (Milano: Feltrinelli 1970)]

Leone, A. A.
1957   "I nomi in -*co* e -*go*", *LN* 18: 87-91.
1959   "Di alcune caratteristiche dell'italiano in Sicilia", *LN* 20: 85-93.
1961   "Gli aggettivi numerali composti di 'uno' ", *LN* 22: 129-131.
1966   "Alcune considerazioni sulla formazione del femminile", *LN* 27: 64-68.

Lepschy, G.
1964   "Note sulla fonematica italiana", *ID* 27: 53-67.
1965   "*k(i)* e *k(i)*", *ID* 28: 181-96.
1966   "I suoni dell'italiano. Alcuni studi recenti", *ID* 39: 49-69.
1969   Review of Muljačić (1969), *Strumenti critici* (Torino) 10: 408-12.
1972   "La grammatica italiana: problemi e proposte", in *Scritti* (1972: 3-13).

Lewy, E.
1942-43   "Der Bau der europäischen Sprachen", *Proceedings of the Royal Irish Academy* (Dublin) C.48: 15-117. [Italian, pp. 39-41]

Liburnio, N.
1526   *Le tre fontane sopra la grammatica et eloquenza di Dante, Petrarcha et Boccaccio* (Venezia: Gregorio de Gregoriis).

Lichem, K.
1969   *Phonetik und Phonologie des heutigen Italienisch* (München: Hueber).

Lichtenhahn, A.
1951   *La storia di ove dove onde donde di dove da dove* (= Romanica Helvetica 38) (Bern: Francke).

Lintner, O.
1962   "Die Kürzungstendenz als treibende Kraft bei der Entstehung von Neologismen in der italienischen Sprache demonstriert an den Suffixbildungen", *Der österreichische Betriebswirt* 11: 202-36.

Lo Cascio, V.
1968   'Struttura, funzione, valore di *andare*+participio passato' ", *LeSt* 3: 271-93.
1969   *Sostituenti e sintagmi verbali. Uno studio su alcune strutture della lingua italiana* (Groningen: V.R.B. - Offsetdrukkerij). [University of Amsterdam dissertation; offset]
1970   *Strutture pronominali e verbali in italiano* (Bologna: Zanichelli). [definitive edition of Lo Cascio (1969)]
1972   "Alcuni sistemi della nominalizzazione in italiano", in *Scritti* (1972: 235-49).

Lucchesi, V.
1972   "Tra grammatica e vocabolario; studio sull' 'aspetto' del verbo italiano", in *Studi* (1972: 179-270).

Lucidi, M.

64

1962 "Prosodemi, tensitività e tensione", *Ricerche linguistiche* 5: 5-15. [reprinted in: M. Lucidi, *Saggi linguistici* (Napoli: Istituto Universitario Orientale 1966), pp. 155-66]

Luna, F.

1536 *Vocabulario di cinquemila vocabuli toschi non men oscuri che utili e necessarij del Furioso, Bocaccio, Petrarcha e Dante, novamente dechiarati e raccolti* (Napoli: Giovanni Sultzbach).

Magnani-Lombardini, S.

1971 "Proposta per un'analisi del nominale fattivo secondo la teoria trasformazionale", *LeSt* 6: 281-93.

Magno Caldognetto, E.

1971 "Ricerche sperimentali sui correlati acustici dei tratti compatto/diffuso e grave/acuto in /p/, /t/, /k/", in *Atti* (1971: 675-81).

Magno Caldognetto, E. - A. Abati - L. Dossi

1971a *Consonanti occlusive sorde e sonore della lingua italiana* (= Quaderni del Centro di Studio per le Ricerche di Fonetica del C.N.R. presso l'Università di Padova 1) (Bologna: Pàtron).

1972b *Introduzione all'analisi e alla sintesi strumentale della parola* (= Quaderni del Centro di Studio per le Ricerche di Fonetica del C.N.R. presso l'Università di Padova 2) (Bologna: Pàtron).

Magno Caldognetto, E. - E. Fava

1974 "Studio sperimentale delle caratteristiche elettroacustiche dell'enfasi su sintagmi in italiano", in *Atti* (1974: 441-56).

Malagòli, G.

1939 "Il problema degli accenti nell'ortografia italiana", *ID* 15: 205-11.

1941 "Intorno al problema degli accenti grafici", *LN* 3: 141-42.

1946 *L'accentazione italiana. Guida pratica* (= Biblioteca di lingua nostra 7) (Firenze: Sansoni). [2nd edition, with a word index: (1968)]

Malmberg, B.

1942-43 "A propos du système phonologique de l'italien", *AL* 3: 34-43.

1962 "La structure phonétique de quelques langues romanes" *Orbis* 11: 131-78.

Mańczak, W.

1967 "Troncamento ed elisione", *BRPh* 6: 114-24.

Manuppella, G.

1952-53 *A língua italiana; guia gramatical para Portugueses e Brasileiros*, 2 vol. (Lisbõa: "Dois Continentes"). [1: *Fonética, morphologia nominal e verbal;* 2: *Palavras invariáveis, noçoes de sintaxe, o lexico, o ritmo e a poesia, espécimes dialectais*]

Manuzzi, G.

1833-40 *Vocabolario della lingua italiana . . . ora novamente corretto ed accresciuto* (Firenze: D. Passigli). [4 vols.]

Marcato Politi, G.

1974 *La sociolinguistica in Italia* (Pisa: Pacini).

Marchand, H.

1953 "The question of the derivative relevancy and the prefixe 's-' in Italian", *SL* 7: 104-14.

1955 "On a question of aspects: a comparison between the progressive form in English and that of Italian and Spanish", *SL* 8: 45-52.

Martinet, A.

01955 *Economie des changements phonétiques* (Bern: Francke).

Mastrelli, C. A.

1951 " 'Bravo', 'bene', 'bello' ", *LN* 12: 111-12.

Medici, M.
1951   " 'Fa fino', 'fa Capri', 'fa 38°parallelo' ", *LN* 12: 91-96.
1952   "Pubblicità quinto potere: osservazioni linguistiche", *Il Mulino* (Bologna)
        10-11: 479-94.
1953   "I prepositivi", *LN* 14: 82.
1959   "Superlativo di sostantivi", *LN* 20: 120-23.
1961   "Alcuni aspetti del linguaggio televisivo", *LN* 22: 119-121.
1965   *Lo sport* (= *Glossari di lingua contemporanea* 2) (Roma: Armando).
1966   "Della preposizione 'su' nel calcio", *LN* 27: 102-3.
1967   *Nuovi mestieri e nuove professioni* (= *Glossari di lingua contemporanea* 8)
        (Roma: Armando).
1969   "Sintassi del periodo della pubblicità", in *Atti* (1969b: 307-18).
1973   *Pubblicità lingua viva* (Milano: Pan).
1975   *Storia e sociologia della lingua. Comunicazione linguistica di massa. Biblio-
        grafia italiana* (Roma: Bulzoni).

Menarini, A.
1947   *Ai margini della lingua* (= *Biblioteca di lingua nostra* 8) (Firenze: Sansoni).
1951   *Profili di vita italiana nelle parole nuove* (Firenze: Le Monnier).
1956   *Il cinema nella lingua; la lingua nel cinema; saggi di filmologia linguistica*
        (= *Collana di studi cinematografici* 5) (Milano - Roma: Fratelli Bocca).

Mengaldo, P. V.
1970   "Aspetti e tendenze della lingua poetica italiana del Novecento", *Cultura e
        Scuola* 36.

Meriggi, P.
1928   "Kymographische Messungen der Expirationsstärke", *Vox* 1928: 1-4.
1929   "Studi di fonetica sperimentale sull'italiano", *ID* 5: 32-65.
1930   "Gli studi di fonetica sperimentale sull'italiano (cenni storici)", *ID* 6: 211-24.

Merlo, C.
1951   "Deverbali e derivati di verbi deverbali e participi accorciati", *Paideia* 6:
        97-101.

Metz, C.
1914   *Ein experimentell-phonetischer Beitrag zur Untersuchung der italienischen
        Konsonantengemination* (Glückstadt: Augustin).

Meyer-Lübke, W.
1890   *Italienische Grammatik* (Leipzig: Reisland).
1901   *Grammatica storica della lingua italiana e dei dialetti toscani*, traduzione e
        riduzione di M. Bartoli e G. Braun (Torino: Chiantore). [2nd edition, edited
        by M. Bartoli: (1927); a more recent edition: (Torino: Loescher 1955)]
1911-20 *Romanisches etymologisches Wörterbuch*, 2 part. (Heidelberg: Winter).
        [3rd revised edition (1930-35)]

Migliorini, B.
1927   *Dal nome proprio al nome comune. Studi semantici sul mutamento dei nomi
        propri di persona in nomi comuni negl'idiomi romanzi* (Genève: Olschki).
        [2nd edition, reprinted with a supplement of i-lxxviii pages: (Firenze:
        Olschki 1968)]
1934   "I nomi maschili in -*a*", *Studi romanzi* 25: 5-76. [= Migliorini (1957: 109-28)]
1938   *Lingua contemporanea* (= *Biblioteca di Lingua nostra* 4) (Firenze: Sansoni).
1941a   *Saggi sulla lingua del Novecento* (= *Biblioteca di Lingua nostra* 1) (Firenze:
        Sansoni). [1942[2], 1963[3]]
1941b   *La lingua nazionale* (Firenze: Le Monnier). [secondary-school handbook]
1941c   "Verso un sistema di accenti grafici", *LN* 3: 69-70.
1943   "Sulla tendenza a evitare il cumulo dei suffissi nella formazione degli agget-
        tivi", in: *Sache, Ort und Wort; J. Jud zum 60. Geburtstag* (= *Romanica Hel-
        vetica* 20) (Genève: Droz; Zürich: Rentsch). [= Migliorini (1957: 135-47)]

66

1945   *Pronunzia fiorentina o pronunzia romana?* (= *Biblioteca di Lingua nostra* 5) (Firenze: Sansoni).

1948   "A proposito dei nomi in *-trice*", *Italica* 25: 99-103. [= Migliorini (1957: 129-34)]

1949   "Il plurale dei nomi in *-cia* e *-gia*", *LN* 10: 24-26.

1949   *Conversazioni sulla lingua italiana* (Firenze: Le Monnier). [2nd edition: (1956)]

1951   *Che cos'è un vocabolario?* (Firenze: Sansoni) [2nd revised edition; 1 st edition: (Roma: La Bussola 1948); 3rd, (1961)]

1952   "Il tipo sintattico 'votate socialista' ", *LN* 13: 113-18. [reprinted in: *Studia Romanica; Gedenkschrift für Eugen Lerch* (Ed.: C. M. Bruneau - P. M. Schon) (Stuttgart: Port 1955, pp. 323-38)]

1957   *Saggi linguistici* (Firenze: Le Monnier). [cf. Migliorini (1934, 1936, 1943, 1948)]

1960   *Storia della lingua italiana* (Firenze: Sansoni). [paperback edition, without notes and indexes: (1963)][cf. Migliorini - Griffith (1966)]

1962   *La lingua italiana d'oggi* (Torino: ERI). [1967^2]

1963   *Parole nuove. Appendice di dodicimila voci al 'Dizionario moderno' di Alfredo Panzini* (Milano: Hoepli). [cf. Panzini (1905)]

1964   "Esiste il neutro in italiano? ", in: *Synteleia Vincenzo Arangio-Ruiz* 1 (Ed.: A. Guarino - L. Labruno) (= *Bibliografia di "Labeo"* 2) (Napoli: Jovene), pp. 307-9.

1965   *Vocabolario della lingua italiana*, edizione rinnovata del *Vocabolario della lingua italiana* di Giulio Cappuccini e Bruno Migliorini (Torino: Paravia). [cf. Cappuccini - Migliorini (1945)]

1968   *Profili di parole* (= *Bibliotechina del saggiatore* 27) (Firenze: Sansoni). [2nd reprint: (1970)]

1973   *Lingua d'oggi e di ieri* (Roma - Caltanisetta: Sciascia).

Migliorini, B. - I. Baldelli

1964   *Breve storia della lingua italiana* (Firenze: Sansoni).

Migliorini, B. - A. Duro

1950   *Prontuario etimologico della lingua italiana* (Torino: Paravia). [1953^2, 195₿ 1970^5]

Migliorini, B. - T. G. Griffith

1966   *The Italian language*, abridged and recast by T. G. Griffith (London: Faber Faber). [= an abridged and recast translation of Migliorini (1960)] [rec.: H (1967a)]

Migliorini, B. - C. Tagliavini - P. Fiorelli

1969   *Dizionario d'ortografia e di pronunzia* (Torino: Edizioni Rai-Radiotelevision italiana).

Mioni, A. M.

1971   "Sistema primario plurimo, sistema secondario italiano. Fonematica contrastiva", in *Atti* (1971: 549-77).

1973   *Fonematica contrastiva* (Bologna: Pàtron).

Mistrorigo, A.

1968   *La liturgia* (= *Glossari di lingua contemporanea* 9) (Roma: Armando).

Moffa, N.

1964   *Formación del plural en los compuestos italianos* (Montevideo).

Monteverdi, A.

1952   *Manuale di avviamento agli studi romanzi. Le lingue romanze* (Milano: Vall

1971   *Cento e Duecento. Nuovi saggi su lingua e letteratura italiana dei primi sec* (= *Officina romanica* Ed.: Aurelio Roncaglia, 18) (Roma: Ateneo).

67

Montaldi, L.
1961   *Autobiografie della leggera* (Torino: Einaudi). [rec.: Valesio (1961)]
Monti, V.
1817-24 *Proposta di alcune correzioni ed aggiunte al Vocabolario della Crusca*
         6 vol. (Milano: Stamperia reale). [reimpression in 7 vol.: (1828)]
Morandi, L. - G. Cappuccini
1894   *Grammatica italiana; regole ed esercizi* (Torino: Paravia).
Mortara, B.
1956   *Studi sintattico-stilistici sulle proposizioni incidentali* (= Università
         di Torino, pubblicazioni della facoltà di lettere e filosofia 8.1) (Cuneo:
         Stabilimento Tipografico Editoriale). [cf. Garavelli Mortara (1972)]
Mourin, L.
1956   "L'imperfetto indicativo", *LN* 17: 82-7.
Musa, M.
1970   " 'Lavorava' versus 'stava lavorando'; the contrast in modern Italian between
         the simple and the progressive form", in Rosetti (1970: 971-5).
Muljačić, Z.
1964   *Opća fonologija i fonologija suvremenog talijanskog jezika* [General phonol-
         ogy and the phonology of Modern Italian] (Zagreb: Udženici Sveučilišta).
         [revised translation: Muljačić (1969)]
1966   "Due analisi binarie del sistema fonematico italiano", *LeSt* 1: 265-79
1967   "Die Klassifikation der romanischen Sprachen", *RJb* 18: 23-37.
1968   "Ancora sull'analisi binaria del sistema fonematico italiano", *LeSt* 3: 41-4.
1969   *Fonologia generale e fonologia della lingua italiana* (Bologna: Il Mulino).
         [a revised translation of Muljačić (1964); cf. Muljačić (1972a)][rec.:
         Di Pietro (1970), Lepschy (1969)]
1971a   *Introduzione allo studio della lingua italiana* (Torino: Einaudi).
1971b   "Gli allomorfi /il/, /lo/ e /l/ e la fonologia jakobsoniana", *LN* 32: 82-4.
1972a   *Fonologia della lingua italiana* (Bologna: Il Mulino). [separate, revised
         and updated edition of Muljačić (1969: 375-564)]
1972b   "Alcune osservazioni sulla gerarchia dei tassemi in italiano", in *Scritti*
         (1972: 253-61).

Nandris, O.
1965   "Problèmes de consonantisme italien et de fonctionnement du langage
         (la gémination, l'allégement des groupes consonantiques, la lénition)", *TLL*
         3: 169-84.
Nef-Reiner, K.
1962   *Aspetti dell'evoluzione sintattica nella lingua italiana contemporanea* (Locarno).
         [Zürich doctoral dissertation]
Niculescu, A.
1967   "Die Struktur der Höflichkeitspronomina in den heutigen italienischen
         Mundarten", *RRLing* 12: 87-142.
1969   "Per uno studio contrastivo dei sistemi fonematici italiano e rumeno",
         Il Veltro (Roma) 13: 287-303.
1971   "La determinazione in romeno e in italiano", in *Atti* (1971: 579-601).
1974   *Strutture allocutive pronominali reverenziali in italiano* (Firenze: Olschki).
Nilsson-Ehle, J.
1947   *Les propositions complétives juxtaposées en italien moderne* (= *Etudes
         romanes de Lund* 9) (Lund: Almqvist & Wiksell).
Noce, H. S.
1941   "The apocopated form of the infinitive in Italian prose", *Italica* 18: 197-
         201.
Norman, H. L.
1937   "Reduplication of consonants in Italian pronunciation", *Italica* 14: 57-63.

68

Olivieri, D.
1953   *Dizionario etimologico italiano* (Milano: Ceschina). [2nd revised edition: (1961)]

Panconcelli-Calzia, G.
1903   "Contribution à l'étude des articulations constrictives de l'italien littéraire", *La parole*, pp. 394-409.
1904   "De la nasalité en italien", *La parole*, pp. 1-110.
1908   "Experimentalphonetische Untersuchungen über den italienischen zehnsilbigen Vers. Beiträge zur objektiven Untersuchung über die italienische Metrik", [*Gutzmanns*] *Medizinisch-pädagogische Monatsschrift für die gesamte Sprachheilkunde* 18: 275-292.
1911a   *Italiano. Fonetica - Morfologia - Testi* (Leipzig: Teubner).
1911b   "Sprachmelodie in italienischen Sätzen und in einem italienischen Gedicht", [*Gutzmanns*] *Medizinisch-pädagogische Monatsschrift für die gesammte Sprac₁ heilkunde* 21: 161-176.
1912   "Über das Verhalten von Dauer und Höhe im Akzent (Italienisch: langer Vokal vor kurzem Konsonanten in einzelnen Wörtern)", *Vox* 23: 127-48.
1921   "Zur Frage der Frequenzbewegungen im italienischen", *ČMF* 17: 125-28.
1939   "Über den 'Frageton' im Italienischen", *VR* 4: 35-47.
Panzini, A.
1905   *Dizionario moderno delle parole che non si trovano nei dizionari comuni* (Milano: Hoepli). [to the eigth edition (1942) an *Appendice* by B. Migliorini is added, separately reprinted as Migliorini (1963)]
Parisi, D.
1968   "Sviluppo del linguaggio nel bambino", in: *I disturbi del linguaggio* (Ed.: L. Pizzamiglio) (Milano: Etas Kompass 1968), pp. 84-151.
Parisi, D. (ed.)
1975   *Studi per un modello del linguaggio (Ia serie)* (Roma: Consiglio Nazionale delle Ricerche).
Parisi, D. - F. Antinucci
1970   "Lexical competence", in: *Advances in psycholinguistics; research papers presented at the Bressanone conference on psycholinguistics*, summer courses at the University of Padua, July 1969 (Ed.: G. B. Flores d'Arcais - W. J. M. Levelt) (Amsterdam - London: North Holland Publishing Company), pp. 197-210.
1973   *Elementi di grammatica* (Torino: Boringhieri).
1975   "Early language acquisition; a second stage", in: *Actes du Colloque internationale de Psycholinguistique* (Paris: C. N. R. S.).
1976   "Early semantic development in child language", in: *Foundations of child language development* (Ed.: E. & E. Lenneberg), UNESCO-IBRO.
Parisi, D. - C. Castelfranchi
1969   "Analisi semantica dei locativi spaziali", in *Atti* (1969b: 327-66).
Parlangèli, O.
1960   *Storia linguistica e storia politica nell'Italia meridionale* (Firenze: Le Monnier).
1971   *La nuova questione della lingua* (Brescia: Paideia).
Parmenter, C. E. - J. N. Carman
1932   "Some remarks on Italian quantity", *Italica* 9: 103-8.
Parmenter, C. E. - S. N. Treviño
1930   "Italian intonation", *Italica* 7: 80-4.
Pasini, G. F.
1968   "Lo studio della metafora", *LeSt* 3: 71-89.

69

Pasquali, G.
1953   *Conversazioni sulla nostra lingua* (Torino: ERI).
1964   *Lingua nuova e antica*, saggi e note a cura di G. Folena (= *Bibliotechina del saggiatore* 20) (Firenze: Sansoni).
Passerini Tosi, C.
1969   *Dizionario della lingua italiana* (Milano: Principato).
Pautasso, M.
1969   *Lingua, dialetto e integrazione linguistica a Pettinengo* (= *Università di Torino, pubblicazioni della facoltà di lettere e filosofia* 10.1) (Torino: Giappichelli).
Pei, M. A.
1941   *The Italian language* (New York: Columbia University Press).
Pekelis, C.
1965   *A dictionary of colorful Italian idioms* (New York: George Braziller).
Pellegrini, G. B.
1960   "Tra lingua e dialetto in Italia", *SMV* 8: 137-153. [= Pellegrini (1975: 11-54).]
1962   "L'italiano regionale", *Cultura e scuola* (Roma) 5: 20-29.
1970   "La classificazione delle lingue romanze e i dialetti italiani", *FI* 4: 211-37.
1972   *Gli arabismi nelle lingue neolatine con speciale riguardo all'Italia*, 2 vols. (Brescia: Paideia).
1975   *Saggi di linguistica italiana. Storia, struttura, società* (Torino: Boringhieri).
Peruzzi, E.
1962   *Problemi di grammatica italiana* (Torino: ERI).
1964   ·*Una lingua per gli italiani* (Torino: ERI).
Pestelli, L.
1967   *Parlare italiano* (Milano: Longanesi).
Petkanov, I.
1956   *La grammatica italiana. Fonetica e morfologia* (Sofija: Nauka i Izkustvo).
Petrocchi, P.
1887   *La grammatica della lingua italiana*, per le scuole elementari superiori (Milano: Trèves). (reprinted [Milano: Longanesi 1952])
1887-91   *Nòvo dizionàrio universale della lingua italiana*, 2 vols. (Milano: Trèves).
Pettenati, G.
1953   "Sul linguaggio recente dei medici", *LN* 14: 24-27.
1955   "Nomenclatura farmaceutica", *LN* 16: 22-27.
Pianigiani, O.
1936-37   *Vocabolario etimologica della lingua italiana*, con prefazione di F. L. Pullè, 2 vols. (Milano: Sonzogno).
Plebe, A.
1966   *Termini della filosofia contemporanea* (= *Glossari di lingua contemporanea* 5) (Roma: Armando).
Politzer, R. L.
1952   "On the origin of Italian plurals", *RR* 43: 272-81.
1955   "A note on North Italian voicing of intervocalic stops", *Word* 11: 416-19.
1958   "On the history of the third person ending in Italian", *Italica* 35: 192-97.
Porena, M.
1942   "Per una più esatta descrizione dei suoni consonantici italiani", *LN* 4: 91-94.
1943   "Il movimento melodico della parola come elemento di studio linguistico", *Rendiconti dell'Accademia d'Italia* 7: 166-84.
Porru, G.
1939   "Anmerkungen über die Phonologie des Italienisches [sic] ", *Travaux du Cercle linguistique de Prague* 8: 187-208.
Posner, R.
1966   *The Romance languages. A linguistic introduction* (Garden City, N.Y.: Anchor books).

70

Pottier, B.
°1958   *Introduction à l'étude de la philologie hispanique* 2: *Morphosyntaxe espagnole* (Bordeaux: chez l'auteur).
Pratelli, R.
1970   "Le renforcement syntaxique des consonnes en italien", *Linguistique* 6: 39-50.
Prati, A.
1951   *Vocabolario etimologico italiano* (Torino: Garzanti). [reprinted: (Roma: Multigrafica 1969)]
Prosdocimi, A. L.
1971   Review of Migliorini (1927 = 1968²), *AGI* 56: 59-71.
Puccioni, G.
1960   "Di alcune recenti costruzioni assolute", *LN* 21: 53-55.
Puglielli, A.
1967   "GN in italiano. Regole a struttura di frase", *AION-G* 10: 189-200.
1968   *The predicate phrase in Italian* (Cornell University). [Ph.D. dissertation] [cf. Puglielli (1970)]
1969   "Complementazione in italiano", in *Atti* (1969b: 367-86).
1970   *Strutture sintattiche del predicato in italiano* (= *Biblioteca di filologia romanza* 15) (Bari: Adriatica). [revised Italian translation of Puglielli (1968)]
Pulgram, E.
1958   *The tongues of Italy; Prehistory and history* (Cambridge, Mass.: Harvard University Press).

Quaresima, E.
1962   "Lingua italiana in bocca trentina", *LN* 23: 20-27.

Raffler-Engel, W. von
1964   *Il prelinguaggio infantile* (Brescia: Paideia).
Ragusa, O.
1956   *Italian verbs: regular and irregular; with a self-pronouncing key and a special guide for the identification of irregular verbs* (New York: Vanni).
Rasi, F. - E. Drago - R. Bruni
1961   "Sviluppo verbale del bambino ricoverato negli istituti di assistenza dell'infanzia", *Minerva Medica* 20.
Regula, M. - J. Jernej
1965   *Grammatica italiana descrittiva su basi storiche e psicologiche* (Bern - Munich: Francke). [Rec. Di Luzio (1967).]
Reinhardstöttner, C. von
1871   *Über die Partikeln der italienischen Sprache; ein Beitrag zur italienischen Syntax und Morphologie* (München).
Renzi, L.
1971   " 'Aveva 55 anni e un orologio da polso' (Gadda): per una semantica di avere", *AGI* 56: 149-64. [= "Per una semantica di 'avere' ", in *Scritti* 1972: 265-279)].
1972   " 'Di' e altre preposizioni", *AGI* 57: 53-64.
Rice, C. C.
1946   "The pronunciation of 'e', 'o' and 's' in Cultivated Italian", *UNCSRLL* 7: 122-8.
Richter, E.
1940   "Die italienischen č- und š- Laute; Untersuchung an umgekehrt laufenden Schallplatten", *Archives néerlandaises de phonétique expérimentale* 16: 1-38.

Rigotti, E.
1972   "Il significato dell'articolo in italiano", *SILTA* 1: 85-132.
Rigutini, G. - P. Fanfani
1875   *Vocabolario italiano della lingua parlata* (Firenze: Cenniana).
Rohlfs, G.
1937   *La struttura linguistica dell'Italia* (Leipzig: Keller).
1949-54   *Historische Grammatik der italienischen Sprache und ihrer Mundarten*,
            3 vol. (= *Biblioteca romanica* 1.5-7) (Bern: Francke). [1: *Lautlehre* (1949);
            2: *Formenlehre und Syntax* (1949); 3: *Syntax und Wortbildung* (1954)]
1966-69   *Grammatica storica della lingua italiana e dei suoi dialetti*, 3 vol. (= *Manua-
            le di letteratura, filologia e linguistica* 3.1-3) (Torino: Einaudi). [1: *Fonetica*,
            translated by S. Persichino (1966); 2: *Morfologia*, translated by T. Fran-
            ceschi (1968); 3: *Sintassi e formazione delle parole*, translated by T. Fran-
            ceschi and M. Caciagli Fancelli (1969)] [paperback edition, in 3 vol.: (1970)]
Romeo, L.
1966   "Sibilants in Standard Italian; facts and fiction in phonemic analysis", *IRAL*
            4: 1-5.
1967   "On the phonemic status of the so-called 'geminates' in Italian", *Linguistics*
            29: 106-16.
1968   "A phonemic inventory of the Italian bivocalic sequences", *FI* 2: 117-43.
Ronconi, A.
1942   "Il presente storico italiano e il suo 'aspetto' ", *LN* 4: 34-36.
1943   "L'imperfetto descrittivo", *LN* 5: 90-93.
1944-45   "L'imperfetto di modestia e l'imperfetto 'irreale' ", *LN* 6: 64-66.
Rosenzweig, A. G. S.
1965   *A spectrographic analysis of consonant length in Standard Italian* [doctoral
            dissertation] (Ann Arbor). [resumed in *Linguistics* 30 (1967): 93-95]
Rosetti, A. (red.)
1970   *Actele celui de-al 12- l ea Congres international de lingvistică și filologie ro-
            manică*, 4 vol. (București: Editura Academiei R.S. România).
Rosiello, L.
1963   "Le sinestesie nell'opera poetica di Montale", *Rendiconti* (Bologna) 7: 1-19.
1965   "Consistenza e distribuzione statistica del lessico poetico di Montale", *Rendi-
            conti* 11-12: 397-421.
Rothe, W.
1966   "Romanische Objektkonjugation", *RF* 78: 530-47.
Rüegg, R.
1956   *Zur Wortgeographie der italienischen Umgangssprache* (= *Kölner romanistische
            Arbeiten* 7) (Köln; Romanisches Seminar der Universität zu Köln; Genf:
            Droz in Kommission). [rec.: Grassi (1958)]
Rüsch, P.
1963   *Invokations- und Fluchformeln im Italienischen* (Winterthur).
Ružička, O.
1943   "L'uso dell'ausiliare e la funzione del verbo", *LN* 5: 88-90.

Sabatini, F.
1965   "Sull'origine dei plurali italiani: i tipi in -*i*", *SLI* 5: 5-39.
Sabbatucci, N.
1965   *Il linguaggio dei politici* (= *Glossari di lingua contemporanea* 3) (Roma:
            Armando).
Saltarelli, M.
1970a   *A phonology of Italian in a generative grammar* (The Hague: Mouton).
1970b   *La grammatica generativa trasformazionale, con introduzione alla fono-
            logia, sintassi e dialettologia italiana* (Firenze: Sansoni).

72

Sandmann, M.
1968   " 'Possessifs' et 'prédicatifs' ", *RLR* 32: 305-23.
Santoli, V.
1942   "Die Struktur der italienischen und der deutschen Sprache", *Germanisch-romanische Monatsschrift* 30: 106-17. [= V. Santoli, *Fra Germania e Italia; scritti di storia letteraria* (Firenze: Le Monnier 1962), 17-27].
Saronne, E. T.
1968   "Per un'analisi semantico-strutturale dell'italiano: struttura sintattica, struttura semantica e contenuto nella determinazione della sinonimia e dell'omonimia degli enunciati", *LeSt* 3: 259-69.
1970   "La questione dell' aspetto verbale in italiano", *LeSt* 5: 271-82.
1971   "Considerations on the category of aspects in Russian and in Italian", *LeSt* 6: 51-66.
Savić, M.
1962   "Predbuduće vreme u prošlosti u italijanskom jeziku" [Future perfect in past tenses in Italian language], *Anali filološkogo fakulteta* 2: 311-24.
1965a   "Le principali funzioni dell'aoristo serbocroato e del passato remoto italiano. Contributo ad uno studio comparativo", *Ling* 7: 65-75.
1965b   "Koncesivne rečenice i koncesivne veznici u najstarijoi italijanskoj prozi u poređenju sa stanjem u savremenom jeziku" [Concessive clauses and concessive conjunctions in the oldest Italian prose, as against the contemporary situation], *Živi jezici* 7: 33-45.
1966   *Temporalni kondicional u italjianskom jeziku* [Temporal conditional in the Italian language] (= *Filoloski fakultet Univerziteta u Beogradu, Monografije* 7) (Beograd).
Scalise, S.
1971   "Problemi di fonologia. A proposito di due libri recenti", *LeSt* 6: 263-80.
Schiaffini, A.
1953   *Momenti di storia della lingua italiana* (Roma: Studium).
1961   *I mille anni della lingua italiana* (Milano: Scheiwiller).
Schmitt-Jensen, J.
1970   *Subjonctif et hypotaxe en italien: une esquisse de la syntaxe du subjonctif dans les propositions subordonnées en italien contemporain* (Odense: Odense University Press). [rec. Herczeg (1972b)]
Schuchardt, H.
1876   "Le redoublement des consonnes en italien dans les syllabes protoniques", *R* 6: 593-4.
Schwarze, Chr.
1967   "Bemerkungen zur Transformationsgrammatik der italienischen Nominalsuffixe", *FoL* 1: 49-58.
1972   "Riflessioni preliminari su un progetto per una nuova grammatica italiana", in *Scritti* (1972: 59-66).
Sciarone, B.
1969   "La place du sujet avant ou après le verbe en italien", *VR* 28: 118-35.
1970   *La place de l'adjectif en italien moderne* (= *Janua Linguarum, series practica* 149) (The Hague: Mouton). [rec.: Telmon (1971)]
Scritti
1972   *Scritti e ricerche di grammatica italiana* (Trieste: Lint). [Proceedings of the two first conferences - December 1969 and February 1971 - of the Centro per lo studio dell'insegnamento all'estero dell'italiano, sponsored by the Università degli studi di Trieste]
Segre, C.
1963a   *Lingua, stile e società. Studi sulla storia della prosa italiana* (Milano: Feltrinelli).

1963b   "Le caratteristiche della lingua italiana", in: C. Bally, *Linguistica generale e linguistica francese* (Milano: Il Saggiatore), pp. 439-70.

Seuren, P. A. M.
1971   "Qualche osservazione sulla frase durativa e iterativa in italiano", in *Atti* (1971: 209-24).

Sigg, M.
1954   *Die Diminutivsuffixe im Toskanischen* (= *Romanica Helvetica* 16) (Bern: Francke).

Škerlj, S.
1966   " 'Come colui che' - formule italienne pour exprimer la causalité", *CFS* 23: 165-73.

Skubic, M.
1965   "Il preterito nel toscano parlato", *Ling* 7: 85-90.
1966-68   "Il valore del piuccheperfetto nella lingua della stampa italiana contemporanea", *Ling* 8: 105-14.
1968   "Il valore del piuccheperfetto nella prosa italiana contemporanea", in Rosetti (1970 1: 487-95).

Sobrero, A.
1971   "Effetti linguistici dei mezzi di comunicazione di massa", *Parole e metodi* 2: 167-89.

Sorrento, L.
1950   *Sintassi romanza; ricerche e prospettive* (Milano: Istituto Editoriale Cisalpino). [1st edition: Torino (1949)]

Sozzi, B. T.
1955   *Aspetti e momenti della questione linguistica* (Padova: Liviana).

Spitzer, L.
1921   *Italienische Kriegsgefangenenbriefe. Materialien zu einer Charakteristik der volkstümlichen italienischen Korrespondenz* (Bonn: Hanstein).
1922   *Italienische Umgangssprache* (Bonn - Leipzig: Schroeder).

Stobitzer, H.
1968   *Aspekt und Aktionsart im Vergleich des Französischen mit dem Deutschen, Englischen und Italienischen* (Tübingen: [Photodruck Präzis]). [dissertation]

Stoppato, L.
1887   *Fonologia italiana* (Milano: Hoepli).

Strohmeyer, F.
1950   "Der Konjunktiv im indirekten Fragesatz im Italienischen", *RJb* 3: 298-314.

Studi
1971   *Studi di grammatica italiana a cura dell'Accademia della Crusca* 1 (Firenze: Sansoni).

Stussi, A.
1969   "Aspetti del linguaggio poetico di Giovanni Pascoli", *ASNSP* 38. 1-37.
1972   "Lingua, dialetto e letteratura", in: R. Romano - C. Vivanti (red.), *Storia d'Italia* 1: *I caratteri originali* (Torino : Einaudi), pp. 677-728.

Sugeta, S.
1966   "The syntagma Noun + Noun in Modern Italian", *Bulletin of the Institute of language teaching* (Tokyo 5: 33-79, 145-46. [Japanese with English summary]

Swanson, P.
1968   *The nominal phrase in Italian. A transformational approach* (Cornell University). [Ph. D. thesis]

Tagliavini, C.
1955-57   *Un nome al giorno; origine e storia di nomi di persona italiani*, 2 vol. (Torino: Edizioni Rai-Radiotelevisione italiana). [reprint: (Bologna: Pàtron 1972)]

74

1963 *Storia di parole pagane e cristiane attraverso i tempi* (Brescia: Morcelliana).
1965 *La corretta pronuncia italiana. Corso discografico di fonetica e ortoepia*
    (Bologna: Capitol). [with 26 33 1/3 rpm records]
1969 "Applicazione dei calcolatori elettronici alla analisi e alla statistica linguistica",
    in: *Automazione*, pp. 111-18.
1972 *Le origini delle lingue neolatine; introduzione alla filologia romanza*[6] (Bologna:
    Pàtron). [1 st edition, mimeographed: (1949); 1952[2]; 1959[3]; 1964[4]]
1976 *Scritti linguistici*, a cura di M. Cortelazzo, G. B. Pellegrini, F. Peruzzi (Bologna:
    Pàtron). [To appear]
Tagliavini, C. - A. M. Mioni
1972 *Cenni di trascrizione fonetica dell'italiano* (Bologna: Pàtron).
Tekavčić, P.
1963 "Un problema della fonematica italiana: la variazione *s / ts* ", *SRAZ* 15-16:
    99-114.
1967 "Sulla motivazione nella formazione delle parole", *SRAZ* 23: 87-102.
1968a "Sull'analisi morfematica di un tipo di derivati italiani; il problema dei cosid-
    detti interfissi", *SRAZ* 25-26: 69-85.
1968b "Il fattore morfematico nelle grafie 'ho', 'hai', 'ha', 'hanno' ", *SRAZ* 25-26:
    103-108.
1968c "Sur le superlatif italien et roman", *SRAZ* 25-26: 23-42.
1970a "Saggio di un'analisi del sistema verbale italiano", *LeS* 5: 1-23.
1970b "Concetti negativi nella formazione delle parole dell'italiano d'oggi", *BRPh* 9:
    279-303.
1970-71 "Attrazione formale e contatto semantico", *SRAZ* 29-32: 55-64.
1972 *Grammatica storica dell'italiano*, 3 vol. (Bologna: Il Mulino). [1: *Fonematica*;
    2: *Morfosintassi*; 3: *Lessico*]
Telmon, T.
1971 Review of Sciarone (1970), *Parole e metodi* 2: 255-58.
Tollemache, F.
1945 *Le parole composte della lingua italiana* (Roma: Rores). .
1954 *I deverbali italiani* (= *Biblioteca di Lingua nostra* 10) (Firenze: Sansoni).
Tommaseo, N. - B. Bellini - G. Meini
1861-79 *Dizionario della lingua italiana nuovamente compilato con oltre centomila
    giunte ai precedenti dizionari, raccolte da Niccolò Tommaseo, G. Campi,
    G. Meini, P. Fanfani*, 8 vol. (Torino: Pomba).
Trabalza, C.
1908 *Storia della grammatica italiana* (Milano: Hoepli). [reprinted: (Bologna: For-
    ni 1963)]
Trabalza, C. - E. Allodoli
1934 *La grammatica degli italiani* (Firenze: Le Monnier). [1934[2,3], 1935[4], 1939[6], 19
Trager, G.
1939 "Comment on Italian e's and o's", *Italica* 16: 145.
Traversetti Andreani, B.
1973 *Le strutture del linguaggio poetico* (Torino: Edizioni Rai-Radiotelevisione
    italiana).
Treves, M.
1947 "Remarks on Italian phonetics", *Italica* 24: 62-68.

Urciolo, R. G.
1965 *The intervocalic plosives in Tuscan (-P-T-C-)* (= *Romanica Helvetica* 74)
    (Bern: Francke).

Valesio, P.
1961 Review of Montaldi (1961), *QIGB* 6: 189-98.

1967a   *Strutture dell'allitterazione. Grammatica, retorica e folklore verbale* (Bologna: Zanichelli).

1967b   "Geminate vowels in the structure of contemporary Italian", *Lingua* 18: 251-70.

1967c   "Suffissi aggettivali fra l'inglese e l'italiano", *LeSt* 2: 357-68.

1967d   Review of Franceschi (1965), *RPh* 21: 92-95.

1968   "The Romance synthetic future pattern and his first attestations", *Lingua* 20: 113-61, 297-307.

1969   "La genesi del futuro romanzo", *LeSt* 4: 405-412.

1971a   "La grammatica della sibilante in italiano", *FI* 5: 226-43.

1971b   "Osservazioni sui verbi attivi e i verbi passivi", in *Atti* (1971: 225-45).

Vaughan, H. H.

1926   "The partitive construction in Italian", *Italica* 3: 5-6.

Vidos, B. E.

1959   *Manuale di linguistica romanza* (Firenze: Olschki).

Vitale, M.

1960   *La questione della lingua* (Palermo: Palumbo).

Vocabolario

1612   *Vocabulario degli Accademici della Crusca* (Venezia: Accademia della Crusca).

1829-40   *Vocabolario universale italiano, a cura della Società tipografica Tramater & C.* (Napoli: Tramater). [2nd edition: (Mantova 1845-56); 3rd edition: (Milano 1878)]

1941   *Vocabolario della lingua italiana* 1: *A-C* (Ed.: Accademia d'Italia) (Milano: Stucchi).

Vockeradt, H.

1878   *Lehrbuch der italienischen Sprache* für die oberen Klassen höherer Lehranstalten und zum Privatstudium 1: *Grammatik der italienischen Sprache* (Berlin: Weidmann).

Volterra, V.

1972   "Il 'no'; prime fasi di sviluppo della negazione nel linguaggio infantile", *Archivio di psicologia, neurologia e psichiatria* 33: 16-52.

Vuolo, E.

1954   "Vocabolari etimologici italiani", *CultNeol* 14: 99-129.

Wandruszka, M.

1958   "Neubelebung des Partizipiums auf '-ante', '-ente', '-iente' ", in: *Romanica; Festschrift für Gerhard Rohlfs* (Ed.: H. Lausberg - H. Weinrich) (Halle: Niemeyer), pp. 481-84.

Wartburg, W. von

1936   *La posizione della lingua italiana nel mondo neolatino* (Leipzig). [reprint: (Firenze: Sansoni 1939)]

Widɫak, S.

1970   *Moyens euphémistiques en italien contemporain* (= *ZNUJ* 26).

1972   *Alcuni aspetti strutturali del funzionamento dell'eufemismo* (Roma: Istituto di Cultura Polacco).

Zambaldi, F.

1889   *Vocabolario etimologico italiano* (Città di Castello: Lapi).

Zampolli, A.

1968   "Recherche statistique sur la composition phonologique de la langue italienne exécutée avec un système IBM", in: *Les machines dans la linguistique; colloque international sur la mécanisation et l'automatisation des recherches linguistiques*, Prague, June 7-11, 1966 (Ed.: E. Mater - J. Stindlová) (Praha: Academia; The Hague: Mouton), pp. 159-75.

76

1973   *Studi di statistica fonematica dell'italiano* (= *Linguistica* 10) (Bologna: Pàtron).
          [to appear]
Zingarelli, N.
1970   *Vocabolario della lingua italiana*, decima edizione rielaborata a cura di M. Do-
          gliotti, L. Rosiello, P. Valesio (Bologna: Zanichelli). [Abridged edition: 1973.]
Zipf, G. K. - F. M. Rogers
1939   "Phonemes and variphones in four present-day Romance languages and Clas-
          sical Latin from the viewpoint of dynamic philology", *Archives néerlandaises
          de phonétique expérimentale* 15: 111-47.
Zolli, P.
1971-72   "Note storiche e bibliografiche sui dizionari di neologismi e barbarismi del
          XIX secolo", *Atti dell'Istituto Veneto* 130: 161-208.
1975   "Per un nuovo dizionario storico-etimologico della lingua italiana", *La Ricer-
          ca Dialettale* 1: 279-301.